SACRED CHOICES

SACRED CHOICES

The Right to Contraception and Abortion in Ten World Religions

Daniel C. Maguire

Fortress Press
Minneapolis

Further materials related to this project can be found at:
http://www.sacredchoices.org

Manufactured in the U.S.A.   AF1-3433
05   04   03   02   01   1   2   3   4   5   6   7   8   9   10

Contents

Preface

CYNICS SAY THAT CONVENTIONAL WISDOM is always wrong. That is an overstatement, but there is one case in which it is clearly wrong. Conventional wisdom says that religions are invariably anti-choice when it comes to contraception with abortion as a backup when necessary. This restrictive viewpoint is indeed found in the world religions, and it is a perfectly respectable and orthodox position within those religions—but it isn't the only respectable and orthodox position within those religions. These traditions are richer, more sensitive, and more subtle than we might believe.

In this book, first-rate religious scholars gathered from around the world show that alongside the familiar *no choice* position, there is a solid *pro-choice* position in all these religious traditions. Thanks to a grant from the David and Lucile Packard Foundation, the Religious Consultation on Population, Reproductive Health, and Ethics brought these scholars together for two long working sessions. I have gathered the fruits of their work in this book. The restrictive view on family planning has been well-published. This is the first time the other side has been heard on this scale.

Our goal as scholars is to change international discourse on the subject of abortion. The two sides in the abortion debate need not be so bitterly divided. There are things we could all agree on. We could all agree that there are too many abortions! We could also all agree on reducing the number of unwanted pregnancies, since that is the key problem. We might further agree that in utopia, there

vii

would be almost no need for abortion. And we could certainly agree that this world is not utopia. It is our hope that we all could endorse the moral freedom of women who must sometimes make this serious decision in an imperfect world.

This book shows that the right to an abortion is solidly grounded in the world's great religions. Governments that restrict that right are abusing the religious freedom of many—in some cases, most—of their citizens.

The world religions can be our guides. For all their imperfections, each of them is a classic in the art of cherishing. Each of them faces the fact that life is *the* good and the precondition of all other goods. But the life that is so good also bears the mark of the tragic. Sometimes the ending of incipient life is the best that life offers. Historically, women have been the principal cherishers and caretakers of life. We can trust them with these decisions. This book shows that the world's religions urge us to do so.

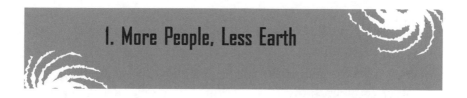

1. More People, Less Earth

WHEN I WAS BORN, only a little more than two billion people lived on Earth. Suddenly there are six billion, with another four or five on the way in the next fifty years. The experts say the population boom will then level off, but no one knows what that number will be. It is worrisome that we have on earth at this time the largest class of fertile persons in the history of the world. Half of the human family are under twenty-five. Depending on what these do, our numbers will peak at mid-century somewhere between nine and eleven billion. Put another way, there are more fertile young folks on planet Earth right now than there were people in 1950, and we have no guarantee about what they will do. World population now is like a triangle, with the reproductive young at the wide bottom and the infertile oldsters at the narrow top. Until this becomes more of a rectangle, with a balance between the young and the old, there will be growth.

There is some good news. Overall population growth has been dropping for years. In fact, some thirty-five nations have stopped growing, and some of these actually have declining populations. Even some poor states in India like Kerala and Goa have stabilized their populations. But world population still grows, because mortality is also declining. Sanitation, food, and medicine are all getting better, and more people are surviving. We're lucky to have been born at this point in history—at least those of us who live in the affluent parts of the world. Prehistoric people only lived for an average of eighteen years, factoring in infant death. In ancient Greece, that figure was twenty, and in ancient Rome, twenty-two. It grew to thirty-seven in medieval Europe and some other parts of the world and was at forty-seven in North America at the beginning of the twentieth century. Extensive child mortality was normal until recently. My father was born in Ireland at the end of the nineteenth century. He was one of thirteen children. Only he and four of his siblings survived into adulthood. When I asked him what happened to the others, he would reply: "One wee girl died of the fever, another wee boy died of the cramps," and so forth. Our family moved to the United States, but my mother would still surprise new parents by saying: "That's a lovely child. I hope God spares her." She was saying she hoped the baby would not die, since, in my mother's experience, a lot of babies— sometimes half of them—did. The old Irish developed a religious mythology to help them live with the terrible pain. When my own son, Danny, was diagnosed with Hunter's Syndrome, causing his death at ten years of age, my mother sought to console me by saying that it was a poor family that did not have at least one angel in heaven praying for them. According to this sad theology, God took away your infants so they could pray in heaven for the rest of the family.

In reality, it wasn't a sadistic God that was the problem. Nutrition and sanitation were poor and medicine almost absent. That's the state of a lot of the world today. You need to make many babies, because most will die. That is family planning of a desperate sort! In Sudan today, many feel they need to have twelve or more children to see three or four survive. Often more than three or four survive. Women are viewed primarily as potential mothers, and so early teenage marriages are often the norm. There is a clear link between illiteracy among girls and women and high birth rates. Also, in many poor countries, children may be the only social security people have, and they can be a financial asset on the farm. In 1984, the World Bank reported that 80 to 90 percent of the people they surveyed in Indonesia, South Korea, Thailand, and Turkey expected to rely on their children for support in their old age. An old Chinese saying was that with each mouth comes two hands. These are some of the reasons why 90 percent of the increase we expect as we go from six to ten billion or more will be in the poorest parts of the world.

Dismissing population problems by saying that overall world population will level off sometime around the middle of this century is small comfort for poor nations like Ethiopia, Pakistan, and Nigeria, whose numbers will probably triple in the next fifty years, with economic and political effects that can hardly be imagined. Half the children in Ethiopia today are undernourished; and if Pakistan triples its numbers as expected, it will have about a tennis court of Pakistani grain land per person—not enough to feed its people even a meager diet. In size, Bangladesh is equivalent to the state of Iowa. But it has forty times the number of people, and its numbers are expected to almost double—to about 210 million—by the middle of this century. Those who would sing songs of comfort about the end of the population problem should first imagine 210 million people in Iowa.

And there is another problem. Even when the poor want to control their fertility, they often cannot find the means to do so. According to John Bongaarts of the Population Council, one-third of the population growth in the next century will be due to the lack of family planning that poor people want but cannot afford. It's not that the poor want to have more babies than they can feed. It's just that foreign aid and national governments do not give them the contraceptive help they need, often due to conservative religious influences on the government. Many people believe that contraception is forbidden by their religion, but this book will show that the world's religions are open to family planning, including contraception and also abortion as a backup when necessary. This information has been too little known. Many people, even within the various religions, have heard only conservative views on family planning. It is well known that there are *no choice* teachings on contraception and abortion in all the religions, but there are also *pro-choice* positions in these same religions that give people their moral freedom to make choices in these matters. These liberating views have been hidden away—this book seeks to reveal them.

What Is So Controversial about Family Planning?

Words, like people, have relatives. When you marry one, you may get all those relatives in the bargain—both the good and the bad.

The term *family planning* has a clan of relatives, and not a peaceable clan. To some people, family planning is the cornerstone of feminism, lifting women from their patriarchally-defined role as mere domestic managers, even "brood mares," defined by their parenting potential in ways that men are not. For others, it is a euphemism for abortion, which they see as always an immoral choice. Others believe population problems are caused by poor people, by what one writer a century ago bluntly called "the untrammeled copulation of the poor."

But there are others who see family planning as the sensible wedding of two good ideas: *family* and that alternative to chaos that we call *planning*. That is the way this book sees it.

The human animal is, by definition, the planning animal. So why does family planning generate so much heat?

Because of its relatives. Family planning relates to sensitive issues such as sexuality, the decision to have children or not to have children, the overall health of this fragile Earth, and the delicate problems of sharing between men and women, rich and poor. That is a heavy bunch of relatives. On top of that, governments get in on family planning. They always have. Governments are concerned with whatever affects the common good, and overpopulation—or underpopulation—affects the common good. In ancient times, the governmental worry was not about too many people but about too few. This led to legislation under the Roman Emperor Augustus that penalized bachelors and rewarded families for their fertility. Widowers and divorcées were expected to remarry within a month! Only those who were over fifty were allowed to remain unmarried. Remember that Augustus presided over a society with an average life expectancy of less than twenty-five years. It was a society where, as historian Peter Brown says, "death fell savagely on the young." Only four out of every hundred men—and fewer women—lived beyond their fiftieth birthday. As a species, we formed our reproductive habits in worlds that were, in Saint John Chrysostom's words, "grazed thin by death." Such instincts are deep-rooted. If, as Jesuit paleontologist Teilhard de Chardin wisely said, nothing is intelligible outside its history, this thrust toward reproduction is the defining story of our breed.

The major religions were spawned in a world where our species lived on the scary brink of depopulation. It is not surprising that these religions would be part of the chorus pushing for fertility. That's what the human race needed. As University of Pennsylvania professor William LaFleur says, the ancient religions "turned reproductivity into a mode of being godly. The multiplication of one's kind became both an index of divine favor and a way of receiving such favor." However, we will see that these same religions developed teachings that would permit, even require, a limit to births.

If you stay with this book and read it to the end, you will know more about your own religion (if any), and also about the other religions of the world. You will learn that these religions are storehouses of good sense and wisdom in areas of sexuality and family planning—more than you suspected. And your respect for them will actually grow.

Too Much of a Good Thing

Many of us living in Western countries look down our streets and don't see too many people. We could easily conclude that this worry about overpopulation is bogus. It's not. Too many people in too little space with not enough to meet their needs is a problem. And this is not a new or brilliant insight. Thirty-five hundred years ago, a stone tablet in Babylon gave a short history of humankind. It said that the Gods made humans to do the scut work that was unworthy of the divinities, but that huge problems developed when the humans overreproduced. So the Gods sent plagues to diminish the population and made it a religious obligation for the remaining humans to limit their fertility. This myth represents the earliest record of worries about too many people.

Clive Ponting, in his classic *A Green History of the World*, reports that "All gathering and hunting groups, both contemporary and historical, seem to have tried to control their numbers so as not to overtax the resources of their ecosystem." Protracted nursing was of some help. Other means used were often grim: They included infanticide, especially of twins, the handicapped, and a proportion of female offspring. *Homo sapiens* (a term we humans claim), as far back as we can see, saw that numbers of people and available resources could be in conflict.

Over two thousand years ago, Aristotle sensibly insisted that a nation should not have more people than it can reasonably provide for. Too many people and too few resources spell trouble. Thomas Aquinas, the thirteenth-century Catholic saint, agreed with Aristotle that the number of children generated should not exceed the provisions of the community, and he even went so far as to say that this should be ensured by law as needed! If more than a certain number of citizens were generated, said Thomas, the result would be poverty, which would breed thievery, sedition, and chaos. All this was centuries before Thomas Malthus, in the eighteenth century, famously and pessimistically proposed that the human population is caught in a vicious cycle: The population exceeds the food supply, leading to famine and disease, bringing population back to a manageable level. Then the process begins again. But Malthus missed a lot of things. He did not see how the need for children could be changed by technology and by the move to cities. You don't need as many children in the city as you did on the farm. As recently as 1800, only 2.5 percent of humans lived in cities. By the 1980s, that figure had risen to more than 50 percent. Malthus underestimated the capacity of the planet to produce food; he was uninformed about the multiple influences on fertility increase and decline, and he also failed to see overconsumption by the rich, not the numbers of the poor, as a more crucial problem. There is enough, as Mohandas K. (Mahatma) Gandhi said, for our need but not for our greed. The 2.9 million people in Chicago consume more than the 100 million-plus people in Bangladesh. Seventy-five percent of the world's pollution is caused by the "well-salaried and well-caloried."

More important than the number of people is the fact that a few gobble up most of the earth's resources while others starve. Buddhism and other religions have diagnosed the human problem as primarily one of *greed*. The power-ful arrange things so that wealth goes from the bottom to the top, and they are efficient at this. The United Nations reported in 1992 that the richest fifth of the human race gets 82.7 percent of the world's income, leaving 17.3 per-cent for the rest of the world. The poorest fifth receive 1.4 percent. The shift from bottom to top is accelerating. Under Prime Minister Margaret Thatcher in the 1980s, the poverty rate in Britain increased from one in ten to one in four, with one child in three officially poor. Under Pres-ident Ronald Reagan in the 1980s, the top 10 percent of American families increased their average family income by 16 percent, the top 5 percent by 23 percent, and the top one percent by 50 percent. The bottom 80 percent all lost. The bottom 10 percent lost 15 percent of their already meager incomes.

This shift of wealth from the weak to the powerful is both color-coded and gender-coded. In 1984 in the United States, more than 75 percent of all the poor were either women or children, including almost one black child in two, one in three Hispanic children, and one in four chil-dren under age six. The problem is worldwide. Noeleen Heyzer, director of the United Nations Development Fund for Women, says that throughout the world "poverty has a female face. Most of the world's poor are women and most of the world's women are poor. . . . Girls constitute the majority of the 130 million children who have no access to primary schooling." The World Health Organization reports that 19,000 people, mostly infants and children, die each day from hunger and malnutrition. Hunger-related illnesses swell this number greatly.

There is nothing accidental about any of this. A few years ago I was visiting congressional offices with a citizens group. Before we entered the office building, we noticed rows of limousines parked and double-parked outside—the chariots of the professional lobbyists. With feigned innocence, I commented: "Isn't that wonderful? All those people are in the congressional offices lobbying for the poor!" The problem is not too many poor people; the problem is too many rich people making people poor. No discussion of overpopulation should run away from this fact. With all these greedy arrangements in place, it is sheer iniquity to blame the poverty of the poor on their fertility.

Still, the point not to be missed is that numbers do count. Too many people on a finite planet can be a problem, especially too many greedy, economically comfortable people. But also too many poor people. *Too many rich people* are high-speed wreckers. *Too many poor people* wreck more slowly, but both are wreckers.

So it's not hard to see why governments, religions, and people with common sense are concerned about population. It's also not hard to see why it is a hot topic, since it touches on so many delicate issues.

Payback Time

Through most of history, the rich could buy themselves a free ride. When the industrial revolution blighted many cities with smoke, dust, and ash, leaving the inhabitants coughing and choking on foul air, those with cash could retreat to country homes and resorts and find clean air and water. That has changed. For the first time in history, the problems of the poor can hurt the well-off. There is no more hiding. Those of us who are comfortably ensconced in the garden spots of the world can easily miss that too many people on the earth—even the desperately poor ones we don't see—make problems for everyone else on earth. We are more connected than we suspected. Religions such as Buddhism, Taoism, Confucianism, and aboriginal Native religions have long taught how utterly interdependent everything is on earth. Now we can see how right they were.

There are around a billion hungry and malnourished people in the world. This causes problems that don't stay overseas. "Too many" *over there* leads to big problems *here*. They can hurt us in two significant ways: (1) through poison and disease, and (2) through job loss in the rich world.

Sick and Getting Sicker

Desperate poor people can destroy an environment. More farmland is needed; forests are destroyed. How does this affect us? In lots of ways. As forests are destroyed, microbes need new hosts and move to humans. Microbes and viruses that used to find a life for themselves in the forests have accepted deforesting humans as their new hosts. It's not the tigers coming out of the forest that we now fear. It's the microbes. And those microbes travel. As Nobel Laureate Joshua Lederberg says: "The bacteria and viruses know nothing of national sovereignties. . . . The microbe that felled one child in a distant continent yesterday can reach yours today and seed a global pandemic tomorrow." We talk of the global economy. Global poisoning is also a new fact of life. The poisons of poverty mix with the poisons of the gluttonous rich and are blowing in the wind and falling in the rain and coming home to us in the strawberries and the beef. The words of the ancient Jeremiah take on a fresh contemporaneity. He warned that it is hard to escape the effects of moral malignancy: "Do you think that you can be exempt? No, you cannot be exempt" (Jeremiah 25:29 NEB).

Overpopulation and poverty conspire with the overconsumption of the comfortable to kill our life support systems. We have lost a fifth of our topsoil and a fifth of tropical rainforests since 1950. Topsoil is that miraculous thin layer of earth that supports all plant life. It is literally more precious than gold. <u>We can live without gold. We cannot live without topsoil.</u> The rainforests are natural treasures that provide oxygen, absorb excess carbon, and supply medicine. (Seventy-five percent of our pharmaceuticals come from plants.) We all get hurt when the planetary womb in which we live gets hurt. Professor of ecology David Orr records some of the results of global poisoning: male sperm counts worldwide have fallen by 50 percent since 1938. Human breast milk often contains more toxins than are permissible in milk sold by dairies—signaling that we have so dirtied the world that some toxins have to be permitted by the dairies. At death, some human bodies contain enough toxins and heavy metals to be classified as hazardous waste. Newborns arrive wounded in their immune systems by the toxins that invaded the womb. One report from India is that "over 80 percent of all hospital patients are the victims of environmental pollution." Human consumption is stressing the oceanic fisheries to their limits, and water tables are falling as more of us need to share this limited resource. If present trends continue, we will not. It's that serious.

Jobs and Refugees
As populations rise in small countries, wages go down, and industries move out of affluent countries to take advantage of cheap labor. Industries also find that poor countries do not enforce environmental laws, so they pollute with abandon, but that pollution blows back at us. Acid rains fall on the rich and poor alike—another way that poverty over there affects the rest of us over here. Desperate people also become refugees, fleeing from their

own homes due to poverty or environmental degradation. The wealthy nations now worry about poor people sneaking in or being smuggled across their borders in a desperate search for work. Short-sighted people just want to build walls or tighten immigration laws. But that's like trying to stop the flow of water by jamming the faucet rather than turning off the spigot. The spigot is *desperate need back home*. Ask the Roman Empire. If you have it and they don't, they will come, and walls or dangerous seas will not stop them. The only cure is helping them find what they need at home: jobs, health care, education for their children, human rights—the things we all want and need. And we all would rather find them at home, not in a land that speaks a foreign language and doesn't welcome us.

"The poverty of the poor is their ruin," said the Jewish scriptures (Proverbs 10:15 NRSV). Increasingly, the poverty of the poor is also our ruin. And remember, 90 percent of the population growth in the next fifty years will be in the poor countries. Moral concern for the unnecessary tragedy of world poverty should break our hearts and move us. According to historian Clive Ponting, some 40 million people die every year from hunger and the diseases spawned or affected by poverty—the equivalent of 300 jumbo jet crashes daily—with half of the passengers being children. When you stop to think of it, war is actually an inefficient and picayune killer, no competitor at all for hunger. What war or holocaust ever did anything so huge! But if moral concern for these people does not move us, self-interest should. The effects of their poverty will come home to us. We cannot be exempt.

Population growth is one of the significant coconspirators in this wasting of people and the environment. The environment is our womb. We and the rest of nature form one fragile and precious community, perhaps the only one like it in all the folds of the universe. The life miracle happened here and possibly nowhere else. One thing all the religions of the world agree on is that we should pause daily and be grateful for this privilege. We don't do that. We're not a grateful people. Our lack of gratitude might well be called our original sin, the root of our undoing.

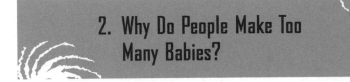

2. Why Do People Make Too Many Babies?

BEWARE SIMPLE ANSWERS TO THIS QUESTION! Simple answers make for simple solutions. Among the simplest—and most wrong—is to say that all we need is more condoms. This ignores the reasons why people—even those with access to contraception—go on making babies anyhow. Family planning that shrinks to just throwing condoms at the problem is a form of self-deception. It ignores the reasons, good and bad, why people feel they need more children. Let's look at just some of these reasons.

According to demographer John Bongaarts's figures, we might add 5.7 billion people in the poor countries between now and the year 2100. By his estimate, 2.8 billion will be the result of "population momentum," the amount of growth if the fertile young simply replace themselves. Those who wanted to use family planning but did not have the means to do it will produce 1.9 billion people. (Many abortions are due to the lack of contraception. That is why it is irrational to deny people contraceptives and then criticize them when they have abortions because they cannot feed more children. They would prefer to have used contraception!) The final 1 billion will come from the cultural desire for big families, a desire that is based on all kinds of things—including religion.

Normally, the desire for children is healthy. It is healthy when you can have children that you can properly care for and when you are bringing them into an environment that is not already overstressed. But there are many kinds of unhealthy and sad reasons for wanting a baby. Sometimes, the desire for children is due to the despair that poverty breeds. In desperate circumstances, studies show, young women find that the only love relationship they can count on is the mother-child relationship. This can prompt them to have babies they are really not prepared to parent. Another cause of excessive fertility is the custom of early marriage forced on girls in their early teens or younger. In Africa, there is a persistent belief that the dead survive as spirits only as long as the descendants remember them. Having many descendants is a kind of postmortem insurance and a stimulus to fertility.

The literacy of women is crucial for sensible family planning. Overall, the literacy rate for women in India is 39 percent, and the fertility rate is almost four children per woman. However, in India's remarkable state of Kerala, the literacy rate for women is 86.3 percent, and the fertility rate is 1.8.

Small wonder that in 1994 the United Nations Population and Development Conference in India saw that the economic and educational empowerment of women is the key to fertility limitation. As Anrudh Jain, a demographer from the Population Council, reports: "The link between education, particularly girls' education, and fertility decline has been established and appreciated for many years." The same can be said regarding poverty. As political economist Asoka Bandarage says: "Fertility declines require alleviation of poverty and improvements in the living conditions of the poor, especially women." Education and the abolition of poverty are essential for family planning. Jain says: "These factors contribute as significantly as contraceptive availability to fertility decline."

So, in a word, family planning requires more than providing contraception with safe abortion as a backup option when necessary. In a true sense, the best contraceptive is hope. When there are hopeful prospects of educa-tion and economic sufficiency, people will manage their fertility in sensible ways.

How Many Is Too Many?

Economist Kenneth Boulding chided his own guild, saying that anyone who believes we can have infinite growth on a finite planet is either a madman or an economist! But really, how big can the human family safely get? Joel E. Cohen, in his monumental book *How Many People Can the Earth Support?* concluded that this is a question that started teasing the human mind in the seventeenth century, when the first estimates were made of the population that the earth's "Land if fully Peopled would sustain." The esti-mate back then was that the earth could support 13 billion at most, and this is not far off from contemporary esti-mates. Most estimates today range from four to sixteen billion. It all depends on what people are willing to settle for. If you were content to live at the level of Auschwitz inmates, the Arctic Inuit people, or the Kalahari desert bushmen, you would get large numbers. If you face the reality that most people today have rising, not lowering, expectations, you get smaller numbers.

The world is not infinite. If the Chinese ate fish at the same rate the Japanese do, it would take all the fish in the world to satisfy them. There are limits. Some estimate that only 3 billion people can eat a diet like that enjoyed in the United States, Western Europe, or Japan. One particularly pessimistic study done at Cornell University estimated that the earth can only support a population of 1 to 2 billion people at a level of consumption roughly equivalent to the current per capita standard for Europe.

Most nations live beyond their means. As a typical example, take the Netherlands. It is estimated that the

Dutch require fourteen times as much productive land as is contained within their own borders. To consume the way they consume takes the equivalent of fourteen Hollands. Where does it get the other thirteen Hollands? It imports from the rest of the world. In one of the great lies of modern parlance, we refer to the gluttonous nations of the world as *developed* and the poor nations as *developing*, implying that they can consume like us, and someday will. But if we can try to return to reality, where in the world is Zimbabwe going to find thirteen Zimbabwes? For all of us to live high on the hog, it would take several more planets just like earth, and we don't have them.

So how many people can the world support? Cohen reaches this sensible conclusion: "The Earth has reached, or will reach within half a century, the maximum number the Earth can support in modes of life that we and our children and their children will choose to want." Family planning is necessary now lest population momentum carry us into chaos, and it will be necessary when the population stabilizes to keep families and overall population at sustainable levels. Family planning is as essential to human life as is reason. As the scientist Harold Dorn says with elemental logic: "No species has ever been able to multiply without limit. There are two biological checks upon a rapid increase in numbers—a high mortality and a low fertility. Unlike other biological organisms [humans] can choose which of these checks shall be applied, but one of them must be." If we overreproduce, nature will kill us off with famine, disease, and environmental destruction. The alternative to that is justice-based family planning.

What Is Religion?

Animals below the human level are neither religious nor ethical. Some can be trained to gentleness or turned into rogues by bad experiences, but in general they work on instinct and genetic instruction. They are programmed to do the things that help them survive. What we humans would call moral duties that help us survive are inscribed in detail on the genes of the animals and insects. It is both our glory and our tragedy that our human genes are not adequately programmed to meet all our survival needs. Instinct and genetic inscription don't do the job for us. With our species, the need is met by ethics and by that powerful cultural motivator that we call religion.

Ethics and religion. It's either them or chaos.

Ethics is simply the systematic effort to study what is good for people and for this generous host of an earth. And before saying what religion is, we can say that whatever it is, we know that it is powerful and a major shaper of culture. Americans are naive about religion. We think that we removed it from public life by passing the First Amendment and separating church and state. The First Amendment was a good idea. Its whole purpose was to guarantee that reason would not be replaced with alleged divine inspiration. After all, divine inspiration was cited to defend the Inquisition, "witch" killings, the Crusades, pogroms, the subjugation of women, and slavery. The framers of the First Amendment said that you don't hand over government to churches, synagogues, mosques, and temples. That's fine, but it's silly to imagine that the First Amendment took that permanent social force that we call religion and threw it out of society.

As the noted historian Garry Wills said, most of the revolutionary movements that transformed, shaped, and reshaped the American nation—"abolitionism, women's suffrage, the union movement, the civil rights movement . . . grew out of religious circles." It's easy to forget it, but if the early Hebrews had not decided that we are all made "in the image of God"—a term that used to be reserved for kings and Pharaohs—Western ideas of democracy would probably not have evolved, and we might not have a Bill of Rights. As scripture scholar Elaine Pagels says, the Bible "forged the basis for what would become, centuries later, the western ideas of freedom and of the infinite value of each human life." Ideas and symbols born in religion have the power to turn society upside down.

Now to define religion: *Religion is the response to the sacred.* So what is the sacred? The sacred is the superlative of precious. It is the word we use for that which is utterly and mysteriously precious in our experience. Since there is no one who finds nothing sacred, religion is all over the place. In the sacred, our experience of value goes beyond all rational explanation. When we talk about the sanctity of life, we are talking about this mysterious preciousness. Let me illustrate this with an example of experiencing the sanctity of life that we can identify with.

Jean-Paul Sartre, the most famous philosopher of the twentieth century, wrote of how he was walking in a park in Paris, late in his life. He met some former students who had their three-month-old baby with them. Sartre took the smiling baby in his arms and was overwhelmed with its literally priceless charm. He said he realized in that mystical moment that if you took all the works of his life and put them on one side of a balancing scale, then put this baby on the other side, his work would weigh as nothing compared to the *sacred* preciousness he held in his arms. This was a religious experience. Now, Sartre was an atheist. He would not explain the sanctity of the baby's value by talking about God, and yet he was responding to the sacred. It was a religious moment.

And that tells us something about religion. Not all the religions we will meet in this book conclude to the existence of a god or gods. Some, like Buddhism, Taoism, and Confucianism, are profound responses to the sacredness of life on this privileged planet. They are filled with reverence and awe, generosity and compassion. They are religious. But they are not theistic. As Chun Fang Yu says, speaking for the Chinese religions: "There is no God transcendent and separate from the world, and there is no heaven outside of the universe to which human beings would want to go for refuge." That is obviously different from other religions like Judaism, Christianity, and Islam, which are confident that there is a God underlying all our experiences of the sacred. Christianity and Islam are confident that we can be united with God after death. Hinduism has multiple gods and goddesses. When it comes to god-talk, there is no unanimity. There never was. How, then, do we all get all these world religions together to address problems that affect all humans?

Answer: We recognize that all religions have a common origin. It is an experience of awe, wonder, reverence, and appreciation of the gift of life in this blessed corner of the universe. Each of the world's religions started there. They then took off on their historic journeys, developing symbols to explain the mysterious preciousness we find here. Their symbols and their rituals of appreciation vary, as do their interpretations of how it all got going. Some are more open to what science says of our origins, some less so, but all genuine religions are expressions of reverent gratitude. Agnostic or atheistic humanism can also be seen as religious, since many who so describe themselves have a rich and generous response to the sacredness of life. Like Sartre, they are deeply sensitive to the sanctity of life.

With all this wild diversity of symbols and differing interpretations, can such a motley group get together on issues such as human rights, ecology, and even family planning? Yes, they can, not by focusing on the differences generated by their march through the centuries but by returning to the primal awe that birthed them all. At the point of reverence for life, we are all at one.

The project that produced this book is proof that religions that are so different in some ways can sit down and talk about common problems. This book was sponsored by a group of international religious scholars known as the Religious Consultation on Population, Reproductive Health, and Ethics. With help from the David and Lucile Packard Foundation and the Ford Foundation, we brought together outstanding religious scholars from ten of the world's religions. Reproductive ethics is complex and multifaceted, and so we brought to the task a group of scholars rich in variety and talent. From Taiwan's Academia Sinica, we have Hsiung Ping-chen, a professor of Chinese cultural history with special interests in sexuality and reproductive patterns. Parichart Suwanbubbha comes to us from Mahidol University in Bangkok, Thailand, to represent the teachings of Buddhism. Riffat Hassan, a native of Pakistan, is a major reforming theologian in Islam. Sandhya Jain lives in New Delhi and studies Hinduism, Jainism, and Indian culture. Jacob Olupona, a native of Nigeria, is an expert on native African religions. Laurie Zoloth heads the Program in Jewish Studies at San Francisco State University. Christine Gudorf is a Catholic theologian teaching at Florida International University. Mary Churchill comes out of the American Cherokee tradition and works on the various native American religions. Beverly Wildung Harrison, recently retired from Union Theological Seminary in New York, wrote the first book by a Protestant on the moral right to choose an abortion, and we drew her from retirement to join our effort. Geling Shang, a native of China, now at Harvard, is an expert on Taoism and

Confucianism. Arvind Sharma, an expert on Hinduism, but also on the comparative study of world religions, completed our group of world religionists. When all is said and done, we have more than ten religions represented here, since there are multiple Native religions; and our experts on Hinduism are also experts on Jainism. Ten, however, is the round number under which we set sail.

To keep the religious scholars informed on the multiple aspects of demography, science, and policy relating to our topic, we were joined by Dr. Anrudh Jain, Senior Director of Policy at the Population Council. Funmi Togonu-Bickesteth came to us from Obafemi Awolowo University in Ile Ife, Nigeria, where she is a professor of social psychology. Dr. José Barzelatto, an endocrinologist natively of Chile, has been an international leader in population and fertility issues for years. At our first meeting, we were assisted by Dr. Oyin Sodipe from the Department of Primary Health Care in Abeokuta, Nigeria.

All of their papers will form the chapters of a book to be published by a university press, but this book now in your hands will introduce you to their work and conclusions and to the work of others in those religions.

Religions Are Changing—They Always Have

Nothing survives that cannot adapt to change, including the world's religions. They have been adapting, correcting themselves, and coming up with new ideas all through the centuries. If they hadn't changed, they would not be taken seriously today. They would be fossils fit only for a mausoleum. For examples of changes we are glad Christians made in their religion, we can look at the Crusades. During the time of the Crusades, Christians thought the greatest thing they could do was to kill non-Christians, especially Jews and Muslims, and religious orders were founded to do just that. When this was going on in the thirteenth century, Thomas Aquinas, in his esteemed book *Summa Theologiae,* said that just as capital punishment of counterfeiters was moral, so too was the execution of "heretics." If we still believed Aquinas, Catholics would be killing their Protestant, Jewish, and Muslim neighbors. Fortunately we got away from that, and modern popes have apologized for some of those terrible wrongs. Does this mean we are perfect now, and no more changes have to be made? Not at all. Some of the coming changes can already be seen.

Let me use Roman Catholicism as one example of ongoing change. In the past, it taught that contraceptive sex could never be justified. We see this changing in many Catholic theologians like Christine Gudorf, whom we will be meeting in this book. Gudorf says that not only is contraception *not* wrong, but that sex should normally be contraceptive and the decision to use sex to have a baby is one that has to be justified. It can be justified if you can give that baby all that it deserves and if you are bringing the child into an environment that is not already overburdened.

Catholic theologians did not talk this way in the past. And it is not just theologians who are changing. In 1994, the Italian bishops issued a report by a panel of the Pontifical Academy of Sciences that stated: "There is a need to contain births in order to avoid creating the insoluble problems that could arise if we were to renounce our responsibilities to future generations." They added that lower death rates and better medical care "have made it unthinkable to sustain indefinitely a birth rate that notably exceeds the level of two children per couple—in other words, the requirement to guarantee the future of humanity." The report recognizes the "unavoidable need to contain births globally." This is a change. Catholic bishops were not putting out reports like this a generation ago.

There are other welcome changes in the Catholic world. The official Vatican publication *Osservatore Romano* published an article in April 2000 by Monsignor Jacques Suaudeau of the Pontifical Council for the Family. In a surprising statement, the monsignor said: "The prophylactic (condom) is one of the ways to 'contain' the sexual transmission of HIV/AIDS, that is, to limit its transmission." Regarding sex workers in Thailand, the monsignor said, "the use of condoms had particularly good results for these people with regard to the prevention of sexually transmitted diseases." He spoke of the use of the condom as justifiable for these purposes—a change in the Vatican's position.

Realistic recognition of the need to plan births is growing similarly in other religions. In 1988, the Grand Mufti of Al-Azhar in Egypt proclaimed it as official Muslim teaching that Islam accepts birth control, and there is also acceptance of abortion in certain circumstances in Islamic teaching. We shall see more of other such changes in other religions. Often, alongside the *no choice* position is a *pro-choice* position that is too little known, even by adherents to the religion. That is the key message of this book.

No religion is a total success story. All of them carry the negative debris they accumulated in their march through time. But the religions we meet here are all at root life-enhancing responses to the sacred. In its distinctive way, each is a classic in the art of cherishing. The study of religion is a mining effort that seeks to bring to light the renewable moral energies lost in the mess we can make of all good things. Good religious studies do not fudge the downside—the sexism and the patriarchy and the authoritarianism abundantly found in religions. Amid all the corruption that accrued to these religions in their long histories, we are searching out the good that survived. And on issues of family planning, the good is there.

It is important to remember that religions are all philoso-
phies of life. Just because you are not actively involved in
any particular religion does not exclude you from enjoying
these treasure troves of wisdom about life and its possibilities. As Morton Smith says, there was "no general term for
religion" in the ancient world. Thus, for example, Judaism
presented itself to the world as a philosophy, a source of
wisdom. Look at Judaism's self-portrait in Deuteronomy:
"You will display your wisdom and understanding to
other peoples. When they hear about these statutes, they
will say, 'what a wise and understanding people this great
nation is!'" (Deuteronomy 4:6 NEB). So, too, the other religions were quests for enlightenment and betterment. They
contain ore that can be mined and refined into rich theories of justice and human rights. Often these treasures
have not been applied helpfully and healthily to issues
like sexuality, family planning, intergender justice, or ecological care; but that is precisely our mission in these
pages. Our particular focus is the human right and obligation to bring moral planning to the human biological
power to reproduce. We are not bunny rabbits or bacteria. We are people, the *animal rationale*, the reasoning
animal, and we have to reproduce in a reasonable way so
that life on this uniquely privileged planet can survive and
thrive.

But What about Abortion?

Both conservatives and liberals can agree: *There are too
many abortions.* In a utopia, there might be almost no
need for abortion. However, all you have to do is open
your eyes to see that it is not a perfect world. It is a world
in which rape, sexual harassment, and abusive sexism are
common. Sex education is often absent or distorted. Contraception is unavailable for hundreds of millions of

women. Grinding poverty produces social chaos, often leading to unwanted and often dangerous pregnancies. To get really serious about cutting back on abortions, all of these things would have to be addressed. We're not there yet.

The religions studied in this book defend what should be the obvious human right to contraception, but they also support the moral and human right to an abortion when necessary. The religious scholars you will meet in these pages are at one with the position stated by Asoka Bandarage: "Abortion should not be used as a contraceptive method, but safe and legal abortions should be available to women who choose to have them. Abortion is, almost always, a painful decision for women. Instead of punishing women for that difficult moral and emotional decision, society should develop compassion and support systems for women in making their own choices." When the difficult decision for an abortion is made, it should be made by the person most intimately involved: the woman. It should not be made by some remote government agency or religious leader. Women have a good track record when it comes to serving and preserving life. They should be trusted with these decisions. We find solid support for this sensible position in the major and indigenous religions of the world.

mostly male?

The need for legal and safe abortion is a deadly serious issue. It is estimated that two hundred thousand women die every year from illegal, unsafe abortions; and the number could be higher, since many nations do not report maternal mortality statistics to the World Health Organization. We work out of the belief that the best way to lower the number of abortions is to promote education and economic well-being, and to make contraceptives available. This is the most effective way to cut back on abortions. This is the truly *pro-life* agenda. <u>Criminalizing abortion is not pro-life; it is anti-woman.</u>

Certain human acts are what I call positive goods. There is no downside to them. Giving food to a hungry person is an example. Some goods can be called negative goods. They are good in conflict situations. They are the best you can do in some cases. Abortion fits into this category. It's something you would like to avoid if possible. You would never say to a young woman, for example: "I wish you a good life, filled with friendship, joy, and professional accomplishment—and to round out your life, I hope you have an abortion or two." No. But you could wish for that young woman the freedom to choose an abortion if she is ever faced with an unwanted pregnancy. The freedom to have the choice of an abortion when needed is a positive good.

In this imperfect world filled with imperfect people, women may become pregnant when they are not emotionally, financially, or physically able to bring that pregnancy to term. Pregnancy, after all, can be seen as a twenty-year condition. Human life is so complex that it takes a lot of rearing and a lot of time to bring a person to maturity. Not every woman who becomes pregnant has the resources to meet that long challenge.

So, one might say: "Why did she become pregnant when she is not ready for it?" Such a question deserves an answer. There are many causes of unwanted pregnancies. Let me list a few: (1) *Ignorance.* The lack of sex education is a fountain of sexual myth about when and how you can get pregnant. (2) *Unavailability of contraceptives.* Sexual passion is a most powerful force that doesn't await the arrival of contraceptives. (Interestingly, the Chinese have started leaving free condoms in hotel and motel drawers.) (3) *Premature sexual experience.* In a culture where sex is constantly being hyped to impressionable young people, unplanned pregnancies will result. (4) What I call the *hostile inseminator syndrome*. The devil here is sexism. Sexism is the belief that women are inferior, and how do you make love to an inferior? Carelessly, would seem to be the answer. Male disinterest in contraceptives is a form of violence. (5) The *surprised virgin syndrome* is another source of mischief. By this I refer to the inability to admit that the relationship is nearing the point where it could get sexual, and that moral choices are called for. Counselors are often told that "it just happened," but that is not honest, since the onset of sexual ardor is, to say the least, noticeable. (6) *Poverty* brings unwanted pregnancies, since poverty breeds chaos and despair and is not conducive to realistic planning in sexual or other areas of life. (7) *Social pressure, especially in the form of peer pressure,* presses young people to begin their sex lives prematurely. The scarlet letter today is *V*, not *A*. Virginity becomes taboo. Too often, the adolescent male sexual impulses make having sex the gateway to social acceptability. This sort of pressure can be seen as a kind of socialized rape. (8) *Alcohol and drug use in dating contexts* removes caution and dilutes good sense. (9) *The diminished influence of religion* with the sexual restraints it included also make for unintended pregnancies. Many religions were too negative toward our sexuality and sexual pleasure and didn't see sex as the sweet good it is, but they also provided cultural brakes that prevented premature or imprudent use of this natural gift.

More could be said, but these answers suffice to show that the question "Why did she become pregnant when she is not ready for it?" is arrogant, judgmental, and naive. As in all matters of gender justice, sexuality, and family planning, both simple answers and simple questions are suspect.

3. The Roman Catholic Freeing of Conscience

WE WILL START WITH THE ROMAN CATHOLIC *positions* (note the plural) on contraception and abortion, not because it is the oldest religious tradition—it is not—but because of its international influence. For one thing, the Catholic Church is the only world religion with a seat in the United Nations. From that seat, the Vatican has been active in promoting the most restrictive Catholic view on family planning, although more liberating Catholic views exist. From its unduly privileged perch in the United Nations, the Vatican, along with the "Catholic" nations—now newly allied with conservative Muslim nations—managed to block reference to contraception and family planning at the 1992 United Nations conference in Rio de Janeiro. This alliance also delayed proceedings at the 1994 United Nations conference in Cairo and impeded any reasonable discussion of abortion. With more than a bit of irony, the then Prime Minister Brundtland of Norway said of the Rio conference: "States that do not have any population problem—in one particular case, even no births at all [Vatican City]—are doing their best, their utmost, to prevent the world from making sensible decisions regarding family planning."

The sudden rapport between the Vatican and conservative Muslim states is interesting. For fourteen centuries, the relationship was stormy to the point of war and persecution. During that time, abortions were known to be happening, and yet this produced no ecumenical coziness. Is the issue really fetuses, or is it that these two patriarchal bastions are bonded in the face of a new threat—the emergence of free, self-determining women? Questions like these and all of the above summon us to visit Roman Catholicism first in our examination of the world religions.

The separation of power and ideas is one of the tragedies of human life. The Catholic tradition is filled with more good sense and flexibility than one would gather from its leaders. Religious leaders are often not equipped to give voice to the best in the tradition they represent. In Catholicism, popes and bishops are usually not theologians, and often they do not express the real treasures of wisdom that Catholicism has to offer the world. Lay people are changing this as they enter the field of Catholic theology and bring their real-life experience as workers, parents, and professionals. Catholic theology is no longer a clergy club, and that is gain.

One of these lay theologians is Christine Gudorf, who will be our principal guide in this chapter. Gudorf is an internationally known scholar teaching at the International University in Miami. She is also a wife and a parent. In recent centuries, Catholic theology was done almost exclusively by men. That has changed, and in the last half of the twentieth century, women began to enrich the tradition with their scholarship and experience as women.

Teilhard de Chardin, the Jesuit scholar, said that nothing is intelligible outside its history. The point is well-taken. If we lost our personal history through amnesia, we would not even know who we are. Gudorf believes, along with many scholars, that nothing clears the mind of caricatures like a bracing walk through history.

The Catholic Story

Gudorf points out that Christianity was born in a world in which contraception and abortion were both known and practiced. The Egyptians, Jews, Greeks, and Romans used a variety of contraception methods, including *coitus interruptus,* pessaries, potions, and condoms; abortion appears to have been a widespread phenomenon. Knowledge of all of this was available to Christians, and although church leaders tried to suppress it, they were never fully successful.

Surprisingly, even before the coming of Christianity, abortion and contraception were not the primary means of limiting fertility in Europe. As it was elsewhere in the world, infanticide was the main method. Christianity reacted against infanticide, but evidence exists that it continued to be practiced. Late medieval and early modern records show a high incidence of "accidental" infant deaths caused by "rolling over" or smothering of infants, or deaths reported as "stillborn." As Gudorf says, "the level of layings over could hardly have been fully accidental."

During the Middle Ages, however, infanticide was much less common than abandonment. Infants for whom parents could not provide were most often left at crossroads, on the doorsteps of individuals, or in marketplaces in the hope that the child would be adopted by passersby. (More often it condemned the children to a life of slavery or an early death.) To ease this crisis, the church in the Middle Ages provided for *oblation*. This meant that children could be offered to the church to be raised in religious monasteries. Many of them eventually became celibate nuns and monks, thus leading to further containment of fertility.

Another Catholic response to excess fertility was the foundling hospital. The foundling hospitals were equipped with a kind of *lazy Susan* wheel (*ruota*) on which the child could be placed anonymously; then the wheel turned, putting the child inside. The good intentions in this were not matched with resources; the vast majority of these infants, sometimes 90 percent of them, were dead within months. Because of the reliance on infanticide and abandonment, it is not surprising that abortion and contraception were not much discussed. As Gudorf says, "the primary pastoral battles in the first millennium were around infanticide, the banning of which undoubtedly raised the incidence of abandonment." The high mortality of children due to nutritional, hygienic, and medical debits was also a common and cruel form of population control.

Catholic Teaching on Contraception and Abortion

Catholic teaching on contraception and abortion has been anything but consistent. What most people—including most Catholics—think of as "the Catholic position" on these issues actually dates from the 1930 encyclical *Casti Connubii* of Pope Pius XI. Prior to that, church teaching was a mixed bag. The pope decided to tidy up the tradition and change it by saying that contraception and sterilization were sins against nature and abortion was a sin against life. As Gudorf says, "both contraception and abortion were generally forbidden" in previous teaching, but both were often thought to be associated with sorcery and witchcraft. In the Decretals of 1230, Pope Gregory IX treated both contraception and abortion as homicide. Some of the Christian Penitentials of the early Middle Ages prescribed seven years of fasting on bread and water for a layman who committed homicide—one year for performing an abortion, but seven years for sterilization. Sterilization was considered more serious than abortion because the issue was not framed as pro-life. Rather, the driving bias was antisexual. Traditional Christian attitudes toward sexuality were so negative that only reproduction could justify sexual activity. Abortion frustrated fertility once; sterilization could frustrate it forever and therefore was more serious. Also, since the role of the ovum was not learned until the nineteenth century, <u>sperm were thought to be little *homunculi*, miniature people</u>, and *male egotism!* for this reason male masturbation was sometimes called homicide. Christian historical sexual ethics is clearly a bit of a hodgepodge. To really understand it, and to arrive at an informed judgment of Catholic moral options, it is necessary to be instructed by a little more history.

Catholic and Pro-choice

Although it is virtually unknown in much public international discourse, the Roman Catholic position on abortion is pluralistic. It has a strong pro-choice tradition and a conservative anti-choice tradition. Neither is official, and neither is more Catholic than the other. The hierarchical attempt to portray the Catholic position as univocal, an unchanging negative wafting through twenty centuries of untroubled consensus, is untrue. By unearthing this authentic openness in the core of the tradition to choice on abortion and contraception, the status of the anti-choice position is revealed as only one among many Catholic views.

The Bible does not condemn abortion. The closest it gets is in Exodus 21:22, which speaks of accidental abortion. This imposes a financial penalty on a man who caused a woman to miscarry "in the course of a brawl" (NEB). The issue here is the father's right to progeny; he could fine you for the misdeed, but he could not claim "an eye for an eye" as if a person had been killed. Thus, as conservative theologian John Connery, S.J., said, "<u>the fetus did not have the same status as the mother in Hebrew Law.</u>"

Following Scripture's silence on abortion, early church history treats it only incidentally and sporadically. Indeed, there is no systematic study of the question until the fifteenth century. One early church writer, Tertullian, discusses what we would today call a late-term emergency abortion. Doctors had to dismember a fetus in order to remove it, and he refers to this emergency measure as a *crudelitas necessaria*, a necessary cruelty. Obviously this amounted to moral approbation of what some today inaccurately call a "partial-birth abortion."

approval

The theory of delayed animation or *delayed ensoulment* developed early on and became the dominant tradition in Christianity. Borrowed from the Greeks, it taught that the spiritual human soul did not arrive in the fetus until as late as three months into the pregnancy. Prior to that time, the life did not have the moral status of a person. Theologians opined that the *conceptum* was enlivened first by a vegetative soul, then an animal soul, and only by a human spiritual soul after it was formed sufficiently. Though sexist efforts were made to say the male soul arrived sooner—maybe a month and a half into the pregnancy—the rule of thumb for when a fetus reached the status of *baby* was three months (or even later). As Gudorf writes, the common pastoral view was "that ensoulment occurred at quickening, when the fetus could first be felt moving in the mother's womb, usually early in the fifth month. Before ensoulment, the fetus was not understood as a human person. This was the reason the Catholic church did not baptize miscarriages or stillbirths."

no science

Reflecting the pious belief in a resurrection of all the dead at the end of the world, Augustine pondered whether early fetuses who miscarried would also rise. He said they would not. He added that neither would all the sperm of history rise again. (For this we can all be grateful.) The conclusion reached by Latin American Catholic theologians in a recent study is this: "It appears that the texts condemning abortion in the early church refer to the abortion of a fully formed fetus." The early fetus did not have the status of *person*, nor would killing it fit the category of murder.

This idea of delayed ensoulment survived throughout the tradition. Saint Thomas Aquinas, the most esteemed of medieval theologians, held this view. Thus the most traditional and stubbornly held position in Catholic Christianity is that early abortions are not murder. Since the vast number of abortions done today in the United States, for example, are early abortions, they are not murder according to this Catholic tradition. Also, according to this Catholic tradition of delayed ensoulment, all pregnancy terminations resulting from the use of RU 486 would not qualify as the killing of a human person.

In the fifteenth century, Antoninus, the saintly archbishop of Florence, did extensive work on abortion. He approved of early abortions to save the life of the woman, a class with many members in the context of fifteenth century medicine. This became common teaching. He was not criticized by the Vatican for this. Indeed, he was later canonized as a saint and thus a model for all Catholics. Many Catholics do not know that there exists a pro-choice Catholic saint who was also an archbishop and a Dominican.

In the sixteenth century, the influential Antoninus de Corduba said that medicine that was also abortifacient could be taken even later in a pregnancy if the mother's health required it. The mother, he insisted, had a *jus prius*, a prior right. Some of the maladies he discussed do not seem to have been matters of life and death for the women, and yet he allowed that abortifacient medicine was morally permissible, even in these cases. Jesuit theologian Thomas Sanchez, who died in the early seventeenth century, said that all of his contemporary Catholic theologians approved of early abortion to save the life of the woman. None of these theologians or bishops were censured for their views. Note again that one of them, Antoninus, was canonized as a saint. Their limited pro-choice position was considered thoroughly orthodox and can be so considered today. In the nineteenth century, the Vatican was invited to enter a debate on a very late-term abortion, requiring dismemberment of a formed fetus in order to save the woman's life. On September 2, 1869, the Vatican refused to decide the case. It referred the questioner to the teaching of theologians on the issue. It was, in other words, the business of the theologians to discuss it freely and arrive at a conclusion. It was not for the Vatican to decide. This appropriate modesty and disinclination to intervene is an older and wiser Catholic model.

What this brief tour of history shows is that a *pro-choice* position coexists alongside a *no choice* position in Catholic history, and neither position can claim to be more Catholic or more authentic than the other. Catholics are free to make their own conscientious decisions in light of this history. Not even the popes claim that the position forbidding all abortion and contraception is infallible. Teachings on abortion are not only *not* infallible, they are, as Gudorf says, "undeveloped." Abortion was not the "birth limitation of choice because it was, until well into the twentieth century, so extremely dangerous to the mother." As our short history tour illustrates, there was no coherent Catholic teaching on the subject, and there still is not. Some Catholic scholars today say all direct abortions are wrong. Some say there are exceptions for cases such as danger to the mother, conception through rape, detected genetic deformity, or other reasons. Gudorf's sensible conclusion: "The best evidence is that the Catholic position is not set in stone and is rather in development."

Sex, Women, and the *Sensus Fidelium*

Debates about sexuality and reproduction are always influenced by certain cultural assumptions. These usually involve attitudes toward women and sex. A culture that looks on women, like Pandora and Eve, as sources of evil is going to have trouble justifying having sex with them; it may conclude that only reproduction can justify sexual collusion with women. That is exactly what happened in Christianity. Augustine said that if it were not for reproduction there would be no use for women at all. In his words, "in any other task a man would be better helped by another man." Early attitudes toward women were poisonous. The Mosaic law assumed male ownership of women. Early church writers said women lacked reason and only possessed the image of God through their connection to men. Luther saw women as being like nails in a wall, prohibited by their nature from moving outside their domestic situation. And Aquinas said that females are produced from male embryos damaged through some accident in the womb. As Gudorf says in her refreshingly sensible book *Body, Sex, and Pleasure*, the church has rejected all of that nonsense but "continues to teach most of the sexual moral code which was founded upon such thinking."

Small wonder that we are rethinking sexual and reproductive ethics. As Gudorf says: "The Roman Catholic Church (and Christianity in general) has in the last century drastically rethought the meaning of marriage, the dignity and worth of women, the relationship between the body and the soul, and the role of bodily pleasure in Christian life, all of which together have revolutionary implications for church teaching on sexuality and reproduction. In effect, the foundations of the old bans have been razed and their replacements will not support the walls of the traditional ban."

Gudorf and other Catholic theologians do not stand alone in the church on this dramatic and important change in Catholic teaching. In 1954, Pope Pius XII laid the groundwork for a change in Catholic teaching when he permitted the rhythm method. Though he quibbled about what means could be used, he did bless contraceptive intent and contraceptive results. He even said there could be multiple reasons to avoid having any children at all in a marriage. In 1968, when Pope Paul VI reaffirmed the view that all mechanical or chemical contraception was sinful, the Catholic bishops of fourteen different countries respectfully disagreed and told the faithful that they were not sinners if they could not accept this papal teaching.

Most of the laity, of course, had already made up their minds. Birth rates in so-called Catholic nations in Europe and in Latin America are close to or below replacement levels. And as Gudorf wryly puts it, "it is difficult to believe that fertility was cut in half through voluntary abstinence from sex." Such dissent by Catholic laity from hierarchical teaching is actually well-provided for in Church teaching. The *sensus fidelium*, the sense of the faithful, is one of the sources of truth in Catholic theology. This means that the consciences and experiences of good people are guideposts to truth that even the hierarchy must consult.

In its best historical realizations, Catholicism is not as hidebound and authoritarian as many bishops, popes, and fearful conservatives would make it seem. There exists dissent from hierarchical teaching that is "in and for the church," as Catholic theologian Charles Curran says. Through much of Catholic history, the hierarchy taught that all interest-taking on loans was a sin of usury—even the smallest amount. The laity saw that this was an error and decided that too much interest was sinful and a reasonable amount was not. A century or two later, the hierarchy agreed—especially after the Vatican opened a bank and learned some of the facts of financial life. The laity are again, along with the theologians, leading the church on the moral freedom to practice contraception and to use abortion when necessary as a backup. Perhaps if the hierarchy were married with families, they could follow the wisdom of the laity in this at a faster pace. It would be a shame if it took a century or two for them to respect the conscience of the laity, graced and grounded as that conscience is in the lived experience of marriage and children.

Gudorf is hopeful in this regard. She believes that within a generation or two, Catholic hierarchical teaching "will change to encourage contraception in marriage and to allow early abortion under some circumstances." She continues: "This change will occur because as the Catholic Church confronts the reality of a biosphere gasping for survival around its teeming human inhabitants, it will discern the will of God and the presence of the Spirit in the choices of those who choose to share responsibility for the lives and health and prosperity of future generations without reproducing themselves, even if that choice involves artificial contraception and early abortion."

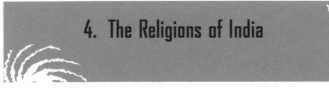

4. The Religions of India

EVERY CULTURE FISHES FOR ITS IDEAS and ideals in certain ponds, ignoring the fishing opportunities in other waters. Europe and the Americas have drawn sustenance from the Greek, Roman, and Jewish worlds particularly, and have profited by this. Judaism, Christianity, and Islam are the three religions that trace back to Abraham (and hence are called the Abrahamic three); these have been influential shapers of Euro-American culture. Much of this influence was positive. Meanwhile, in the rest of the world, human beings through the ages have gotten up every morning and tried, with successes largely unknown to us, to figure out what life means. In India, China, Africa, and beyond, human genius has blossomed in poetic and religious forms that are rich in the understanding of life and its possibilities and delights. These flowerings of culture beckon to us. In the words of the Buddha, they say to us, "Come and see!"

In this chapter, we go to India *to see*. We will see that Hinduism is the main religion, embraced in some way by 80 percent of the Indian people. There is no tidy little creed that sums up Hinduism, and it can be said that Hinduism is more a confederation of religions than a single denomination. Yet in the rich variety of forms that Hinduism assumes, there are commonalities and motifs that are relatively constant.

Meeting Hinduism

I believe the best way to meet a religion is in a person, not in a book or creed. In Hinduism, that person is Mohandas K.

Gandhi, the most famous Hindu of our times. Gandhi is more than a Hindu hero; he is the moral giant of the twentieth century, an unparalleled example of the power of spiritual and moral conviction. He was a slight figure less than 100 pounds, and his possessions when he died were worth less than five dollars. And yet he led the liberation of India from foreign control and taught the world the power of a nonviolent struggle for justice. His sense of justice was fearless. He assaulted the cruelest prejudice in India by naming the Untouchables the *harijan,* the children of God, thus beginning the slow undermining of caste in India.

Gandhi illustrates one of the great beauties of Hinduism: its intellectual tolerance and openness. He studied not just the Vedas of Hinduism but the Bible of Jews and Christians and the Qur'an of Islam, and he actually taught other religions something about themselves. Many of the Christian peace movement's modern leaders found the Christian peace ideal though Gandhi, not through their own religious communities. This was certainly true in the case of Martin Luther King Jr. Gandhi was the moral and political leader not just of Indian liberation but also of the United States civil rights revolution. One Christian writer even said that "the most Christlike man in history was not a Christian at all." He was a Hindu named Gandhi.

Hinduism is open to wisdom from any source. Gandhi said: "I believe in having equal regard for all faiths and creeds." He did not believe there was one true and perfect faith. In the words of the Christian apostle Paul, we all know "in part." In Gandhi's words, "all faiths constitute a revelation of Truth, but all are imperfect and liable to error. Reverence for other faiths need not blind us to their faults." Thus the Laws of Manu are sacred to Hindus, but they say some atrocious things about women. "By a girl, by a young woman, or even by an aged one, nothing must be done independently, even in her own house. In childhood, a female must be subject to her father, in youth to her husband, when her lord is dead to her sons; a woman must never be independent. Though destitute of virtue, or seeking pleasure elsewhere, or devoid of good qualities, yet a husband must be constantly worshipped as a god by a faithful wife." Gandhi said these teachings were simply in error.

The same can be said of the Christian scriptures; the epistle to the Ephesians tells women to be subject to their husbands as if the men were divine. That is as wrong as the Laws of Manu were when they made the same sexist point. As theologian Diana Eck sees it, "religions are not revealed full-blown from heaven. They are human responses to the glimpses of God's revelation, human creations, bearing the imprint of inevitable human imperfection." Some Buddhists go even further and say that every belief system is an illness waiting to be cured. That is a bit too sweeping; these rich traditions contain much positive content. But no matter what religion you study, you will find much that is wrong and harmful. If that were all there was to find, these religions would be useless and discardable. But within these classics are renewable moral energies that have transformed societies in the past and can do so again. To make matters worse, the faithful of the world's religions are not very faithful to the ideals of their religions. As Gandhi said, "much of what passes for Christianity is a negation of the Sermon on the Mount." And the best insights of Hinduism are often mocked by the daily lives of Indians. We are all hypocrites to some degree, professing one thing and doing another.

Having said that, let us agree that any religion that can produce a Gandhi deserves a hearing in all serious moral debates. Our question: What can Hinduism teach us on matters of family planning?

Dharma

Our principal guide in this chapter will be Sandhya Jain. Jain lives in India. She is a student of India's religions, particularly Hinduism and Jainism, and an internationally respected journalist and commentator on Indian politics and culture.

Before getting to the issues of contraception and abortion, Jain directs us to the major teachings of the Hindu religion for the background against which all moral judgments are made. To meet Hinduism, start with *dharma*. Derived from the Sanskrit word *dhr*, it means "that which supports right living" and "that which is conducive to the highest good." *Dharma* is the law of life—the moral or the natural law, we might call it. Sometimes Hindus call their religion *eternal dharma*; that's how central it is. We might be tempted to think that *dharma* is a blueprint that gives detailed, unchanging instructions for the entire moral life. That would be a mistake. Built into the notion of *dharma* is the need to adapt to changing circumstances. Life is always the same, and it is also always different. Morality (*dharma*) has to be consistent but also adaptive. Obligations change as situations change. (Already you can see how this will apply to family planning. When more people were dying than being born, it was good to have more children. When we are overcrowded, *dharma* says, "take note!")

Jain says: "Like a river, *dharma* maintains a continuous flow through the ages, constantly renewing and replenishing its waters (contents) and continually altering its course, while giving the appearance of changelessness." This insistence on the need to adapt to new circumstances,

Jain says, has given "Hinduism its incredible capacity to vary its metaphysical and ethical principles in consonance with the social and historical realities of the day, without losing its essential character or sense of identity." It is true that Hinduism has encouraged big families and has a bias for boy babies. However, Jain says, "this ancient religion is as malleable as it is eternal. This religion can be utterly transformed and turned on its head in the name of religion itself."

Hinduism believes change is non-threatening; resistance to necessary change is a mark of ignorance and futility. Religious reformers can get somewhere in India. Jain says that "by and large, progressive ideas and movements in India have not encountered religious opposition." On the contrary, the successful efforts to eliminate *sati*, the self-immolation of a widow on the funeral pyre of her husband, were led by religious leaders. The same is true for the promotion of the right of widows to remarry and for resistance to Untouchability (in which Gandhi led the way). The ideal of a small family is growing. Religious reformers are challenging the religiously grounded bias in favor of male offspring. It was taught that the eldest son enjoys a special status because he can offer the rites that advantage his departed father in the afterlife. As religious reformers teach that girls can do the same, this is changing. As we shall see, religious leaders have also rallied in favor of family planning.

Karma

Karma is a strong feature of Hinduism and the religions, like Buddhism and Jainism, that were influenced by Hinduism. *Karma* is basically a belief that what you sow, you will reap. And it is not just individualistic. What society sows, society reaps. If India has hundreds of millions of

poor people, it is not an act of God. It is the harvest of
deeds done and duties neglected. Every thought and every
deed has an unavoidable impact. *Karma* is the fate that
you yourself have—or a whole society has—chiseled out.
It is the powerful belief that we get what we have coming
to us, the good and the bad. This fights the human tendency to blame blind fate or chance for social disasters.

We are geniuses at dodging blame. The Black Plague was
blamed on divine retribution instead of the horrendous
unhygienic conditions in which most people lived. Global
warming is blamed on the inevitable cycles of nature rather
than our double-basting the planet in carbon dioxide. The
gobbling up of 80 percent of income by the top 20 percent
of people is just a given; greed has nothing to do with it.
Nonsense, says the doctrine of *karma*. A lot of sowing has
gone on. We are just looking at the harvest.

Karma doctrine is a piercing call to candor. It also
involves faith that real possibilities of goodness exist in
this little corner of the universe. Hinduism has an inner
optimism about our reality. As Hindu scholar Anantanand
Rambachan says, it is Hindu belief that "the divine exists
equally and identically in all beings and things." As the
Bhagavad Gita puts it: "He who sees the Supreme Lord,
existing alike in all beings, not perishing when they perish,
truly sees." In other words, this is a belief that deep down,
in all things, there is a divine spark. Reality is basically
good and promising. This is a hopeful posture. It matches
the Genesis story of the Hebrews that portrayed God as
looking on creation and pronouncing it "very good." This
puts the obligation on us not to mess it up. If poverty is
killing 40 million people a year, don't blame God. Don't
blame this "very good" earth. The enemy is us.

Karma strips away rationalization and shouts a big
loud accusation at the human race. It is a blunt demand

for accountability. Looking at the wreck we are making of the earth, *karma* says "it ain't necessarily so!" *Karma* doctrine is practical. It could be directed now against the prevalent Indian practice of female abortion and female infanticide. This has lowered the ratio of men to women. In 1991, there were 927 women for 1,000 men. In 1901, the ratio had been 972 women to 1,000 men. India is sowing here, and it takes no genius to see what it will reap.

Karma is strongly tied to the belief in reincarnation in Indian religions and in Buddhism. The *karma* that one has accumulated determines how and in what form one will be reborn or whether one will escape the cycle of rebirth and enter a state of bliss. Aside from this belief, however, *karma* teaching stresses the impact of our behavior on this planet.

Ahimsa

Especially through the influence of Gandhi, *ahimsa* has featured prominently in Hindu morality. The word connotes nonviolence and compassion toward all beings. Gandhi took instruction on *ahimsa* from Jainism. Jainism is another of India's ancient religions. Though small in its number of adherents, Jainism has had a major influence on Indian culture and on India's majority religion, Hinduism. That it has had such an influence on Hinduism signals how open Hinduism is to other religious views, especially since Jainism rejects the idea of a God who creates and denies the authority of the Vedas, which have scriptural standing for Hindus. (Jains also reject the idea of caste.) Where Jainism shines is in its simplicity of life and avoidance of selfish indulgence. Jains insist on five major moral commitments, and this pentagon of virtues has also been absorbed by Hinduism. The first is *ahimsa*: noninjury, nonviolence, compassion; the second is *satya*:

speaking truth and respecting the power of truth; the third is *asteya*: not taking anything not given. The fourth also curbs the human desire to own: *aparigraha*, the restriction of the desire to possess and dominate. The last is *brahmacarya*: sexual restraint.

The Jain stress on *ahimsa*, on not doing injury or violence, leads some Jains to reject abortion. In support of abortion, other Jains point out that in some situations, abortion may be the only way to avoid greater injury.

Hinduism on Abortion

At first blush, it would seem that Hinduism is the last place to go if you want to take a pro-choice view on abortion. In the prestigious *Dharma Sastras* and in other major writings, Hindus are told never to practice abortion even in the case of an illegitimate child. Abortion is presented as a heinous crime and is classified as one of the *mahapatakas* (atrocious acts), subjected to severe penances and punishments. Other sources list abortion as the basest of sins, pointing out the bad *karma* it produces that could have negative consequences in this life and the next. Jain notes that this "apparently implacable aversion to abortions derives from the Hindu theory of conception as the result of a divine act, and hence as holy and worthy of reverence."

Conception is not just the material union of sperm and ovum. It also involves the life principle or spirit, the *atman*. The term *atman* is seen as the link with God. "God abides in the *atman*, and the *atman* abides in God." Thus, as Jain says, "in the Hindu view both physical and spiritual life enters the human embryo at the moment of conception itself and there is never a pure state of matter alone." For those who believe in reincarnation, the seriousness is even greater, since the *karma* of a past life will be reentering in this birth. The embryo is not just tissue.

It's a being endowed with spirit, dignity, and a previous history.

The deck would therefore seem to be firmly stacked against the moral permissibility of any abortion in the Hindu world. But abortion has been legal in India since 1971 with the passing of the Medical Termination of Pregnancy Act! This law permits abortion in cases of rape, incest, and even for the mental health of the woman if she would be adversely affected by the birth of an unwanted child. "With such broad-ranging provisions," says Jain, "it can easily be seen that in India, abortion is available practically on demand." Moreover, the Indian government is planning to extend the Termination of Pregnancy Act to provide abortion rights to minor girls below 18 years of age, whether married or unmarried, without the consent of their guardians. And, remarkably, says Jain, "Hindu religious bodies have not expressed any opposition to this move." And Hindu religious bodies are not bashful about speaking out on any moral issue.

How then can we explain this stunning inconsistency? Is this another case of East is East, West is West, and never the twain shall meet? Is there something in the "inscrutable East" that others could never understand?

Not really.

Better Insights Replacing Old Taboos

Religions developed when illiteracy was the norm, and their teachers often taught the way parents teach toddlers. They used absolutes, not nuanced rules. You don't say to a toddler: "It would be ideal if you never crossed the street. However, there may be circumstances in which there is no danger, and you may have good reasons to cross by yourself on your own authority. " No, we say: "Don't you dare ever go out into that street." This tendency to use absolute commands endures in most religions. They continue to treat adults like unlettered and unthinking children. That Hindu teachers are not complaining about these changes in abortion laws, allowing people to make their own decisions, puts them a step ahead of the Vatican. Hindu teachers are showing respect for the mature consciences of their people. The Vatican is still enmeshed in the parental control syndrome: "Don't you dare!"

So East and West are not that far apart when it comes to morality and change. We can even find an example in Catholic Italy of this kind of adaptability. In the 1950s, I was a Catholic seminarian studying in Rome. When Lent arrived my first year there, I found in the official rules of the church that fasting and abstinence from meat were required every day in Lent. Yet what to my wondering Irish Catholic eyes should appear but the obvious fact that no one—priest or layperson—was fasting or abstaining. I even went to the extent of calling the Vicariate, the church headquarters in Rome. The impatient voice of some monsignor, who clearly wished he had not answered this call, received my question: "Do we have to fast and abstain during Lent?"

With a suppressed moan, he replied, "No." Then he added as an afterthought, "Maybe on Ash Wednesday and Good Friday."

Having heard that "maybe," I pressed him: "But do we *really* have to fast on those two days?"

"No," he replied, and quickly bid me good day.

What was going on here? Italy had just gone through a terrible war during which finding food, not fasting and abstaining, was the issue. On top of that, Catholicism had been rediscovering the biblical stress on social justice and care for the poor as much more important than dietary restrictions. Even the bishops of the church eventually changed the fasting laws and caught up with the laity. The same thing that Christine Gudorf has predicted for birth control took place. Better insights replaced old taboos.

There is another reason why Hinduism can allow for the choice of abortion. Religious traditions are never seamless garments, though the faithful like to think of them that way. They are patchwork quilts, and not all the patches match. Alongside the prohibitions against abortion, ample evidence exists in the ancient medical texts of India that contraception and abortion were going on. As Jain says: "These all attest to the fact that there has always been a human need to control or mitigate the consequences of sexuality, and that this fact was recognized, with sympathy, by at least a section of the religious-medical teachers at various times." In fact, the strong condemnations of abortion mentioned above indicate that those inveighing against them had something to inveigh against. Abortion was approved by some and practiced by many—otherwise it would not have won a place in the medical treatises. This is one of the same reasonable arguments used by Christian scholars to show that women had leadership roles in the early church. All the virulent condemnations of women's participation would have been unnecessary if the women had not been asserting themselves.

In Praise of Small Families

Alongside the Vedas' lauding of the family with "ten sons," the ideal of the small family persists in the complex tapestry of Hinduism. Epic stories do much Hindu moral teaching. The famous epic *Mahabharat* offers great praise for the Pandavas, who served as one of the Hindu prototypes of the ideal family. The Pandavas have small families and are exemplary in meeting the exacting demands of *dharma*. Their enemies the Kauravas have large families but are not treated as righteous. Small families are praised. Of Rama's wife Sita and her three sisters, it was written: "Two beautiful sons had Sita . . . Two sons did all the mothers give birth to, all beautiful, graceful, and full of virtue." Jain comments: "In almost all cultures, the Holy Family tends to be a small family." The "big hint" in the Hindu tradition, she says, is that this not only promotes material well-being but spiritual growth as well.

Arguments for family planning can be drawn from the main moral teachings of Hinduism and Jainism. *Dharma* emphasizes a need to act "for the sake of the good of the world." In other words, *dharma* includes a social conscience and a concern for how our individual choices affect the common good. It includes a sense of the interrelatedness of all forms of life. Producing more children than you or the environment can support is not "for the sake of the good of the world" but is a harmful form of greed. It violates the "five vows": (1) *ahimsa,* which encourages nonviolence and avoiding harm (greed can harm children, ecology, and society); (2) *satya,* which is truthfulness (pregnancy is a promise you should be able to fulfill truthfully); (3) *brahmacarya,* which encourages bringing reasonable restraints to the use of sexuality (this is violated); and (4) *asteya* and (5) *aparigraha,* which forbid stealing and greedy possessiveness and encourage frugality. Overpopulating beyond your means or society's capacity is claiming more than you have a right to. It is profligacy, not frugality. There is no kindness or compassion in it. It violates *ahimsa* and all the other moral commitments.

Lessons From Kerala

Kerala is one of the poorest states in India, but it can teach the world. Its great lesson on family planning is that family planning is next to useless if it only provides contraceptives with abortion as a backup. Kerala is a success story in fertility management, and the story it tells is that *the solution calls for more than condoms.* Simply, it calls for social justice. But let's spell out the details of Kerala's formula of success.

Kerala's population density is three times India's average, but its recent fertility decline is unparalleled in any comparable state. Statistics sometimes tell the truth. Look at these: The total fertility rate in India is 3.56; in Kerala, 1.8. The replacement fertility rate is thought to be 2.1 per woman. Infant mortality in Kerala is well below the average in the rest of India. Literacy for women in India is 39 percent; in Kerala, 86.3 percent and climbing. The percentage of people living below the poverty line in India is 40; in Kerala, 27. Female age at first marriage is 18.7 in India but 22 in Kerala, and fully 22 percent of women in Kerala never marry. These marriage statistics certainly relate to the economic opportunities available to educated women.

Add to the above the availability of universal primary education in Kerala, minimum wage and child labor laws, improving medical facilities, and the likelihood that children will survive into adulthood. Under such circumstances, as anthropologist Joan Mencher has said, even poor agricultural laborers become "amenable to family planning." But notice: If people are not "amenable to family planning," families are not planned. And people become amenable when they live in a society marked by hope and justice. This is the message Kerala sends, not only to the rest of India, but to the world.

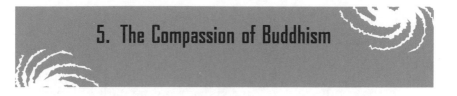

5. The Compassion of Buddhism

MOST RELIGIONS BEGIN WITH SIMPLE IDEAS and understandable ideals. Then the scholars go to work, and the
original enlivening spirit can be lost in jargon and gib-
berish. Look at Jesus' Sermon on the Mount, the Magna
Charta of his religious movement. Then look at some of
the subsequent theological treatises on "circuminsession
and the subsistent relations of the Trinity"; it is not a feat
of clarity. (Jesus himself would have trouble understanding it.) Buddhism suffered the same fate. One scholar,
after reporting on the basic doctrine of Buddhism, commented: "This very simple doctrine was developed in various rather pedantic forms, most important of which was
the 'Chain of Dependent Origination' . . . commented on
again and again by ancient and modern scholars, and
probably not fully understood by anybody." That's a
rare statement. Scholars are usually not that honest
about the knavish obscurity to which their kind are all
too prone.

Buddhism, like Christianity, had simple and refreshing
beginnings. The Buddha lived 2,500 years ago in what
today is Nepal. He discovered a way of life that was simple and balanced. He called it "the *Middle Way*." Somewhere between manic self-indulgence and grim mortifica-
tion there lies the middle way of moderation. The Buddha
sensed that we can easily get caught in the treadmill of
greedy grabbing and of never knowing the elusive good
news that "enough is enough." What we don't have can
blind us to what we have.

Let's take a look at the basic catechism of Buddhism. We might see why Buddhism is a growing religion today, one that brings the cool waters of relief to our fevered and hyperactive modern lives. But Buddhism is not a major religion just because it has led many on the path of inner peace. It has also distinguished itself by its conviction that humans can undergo major transformation. Buddhism moved into a Tibet in which warriors were the ideal and changed society over time so that monks became the ideal. Three hundred years before the birth of Jesus, the Buddhist king Asoka put Buddhism into practice and changed a society focused on militarism and greed into a society of relative peacefulness. Buddhism has a track record, and that is one more reason to give it a listen. The Buddha's insights begin with what have been called the Four Noble Truths.

The Four Noble Truths

Suffering exists.

Much suffering in societies and in individual persons arises from excessive and unrealistic desires.

When attachment to such desires ceases, suffering abates.   people?

This relief from suffering is cultivated by practicing the Eight-fold Path of the Middle Way.

The purpose of the *Eight-fold Path of the Middle Way* is to make us truly peaceful and happy. The eight ways of the path are Right View, Right Motives, Right Speech, Right Action, Right Livelihood, Right Effort, Right Mindfulness, and Right Contemplation. This list might sound too vague to be meaningful, but take a look at what it is saying. Each of the eight ways has a specific content.

Right View means recognizing that all things and all people are *interdependent and linked*. Most of us are ignorant of how interlocked we are with everyone and everything else. Science confirms Buddhism here by saying that all life—including us, the birds, the bees, the flowers, and the viruses!—all evolved from a single cell. Otherwise the basic biological similarity could not be accounted for. The birds and animals and roses are our siblings. It's not poetry so much as fact to say that all that lives is family. You can see right away what this can do for ecological awareness—and for family planning. No species in the community of life should overreproduce and destroy the rest of life.

When Buddhism says that all being is interbeing—all that is, is related—it is not saying that all of life is of equal value. People are worth more than mosquitoes. Human life is a higher realization of life, but it is kin to the rest of it. We had a common origin. Also, we are part of the universe. The cells in our hands and face were once stardust, and will be so again when our sun runs out of energy and this earth dissolves. We can truly adapt the old Catholic mantra: "Stardust thou art and unto stardust thou shalt return." Ecologist John Seed reminds us that we are related to everything, including the rocks. We should look at our bodies and remember that "Every atom in this body existed before organic life emerged 4000 million years ago. Remember our childhood as minerals, lava, as rocks? We are the rocks dancing. Why do we look down on them with such a condescending air? It is they that are the immortal part of us." Recognizing all of that, says the Buddha, is the Right View. It's the realistic perspective from which we start.

Right Motives refers to being honest and thoughtful about your real intentions. Is your lifestyle honorable, or does it make you a predator? To quote Gandhi again, there is enough on this earth for our need but not for our greed. It's not love of life or love of children that makes our species produce more children than the earth can support. Rarely do we, who gobble up more than our share, sit down and ponder our real motives. It's too scary. We might just discover the kind of people we are. Buddhism dares us to think about it, adding that we won't really be at peace with ourselves until we do.

Right Speech targets deceit and lying. It's deceitful to think that all is well because all looks well from our patio. Our minds are drenched in deceit by advertising and the modern media. I remember when my son Tom was five years old. He came running into the kitchen to tell me that a certain soap gets your clothes cleaner than all the other soaps. I asked him who told him that. "The man on television," he said, eyes wide open and full of unquestioning faith. I said: "He might not be telling the truth." "What!?" said Tom, as his mouth dropped open in total shock. His first loss of innocence! The television and all the media feed us deceit. More money is spent on advertising than on higher education in the United States, and truth is not the bottom line. Buddhism joins Christianity in saying "the truth will make you free."

Right Action says avoid killing, stealing, harmful sexual behavior, lying, and harmful intoxicants. (We might at this point wonder how Buddhists who are so against killing and are so strongly for peace—there has never been a Buddhist Holy War!—can still support abortion when necessary. We'll get to this shortly.)

Right Livelihood means earning your living in ways that do no harm to other living beings or to the environment. *Right Effort* goes after the big human weaknesses, the ones that most disrupt our inner peace and our society: *greed, gluttony, hatred, anger, and delusion. Right Mindfulness* and *Right Contemplation* urge us to stop, look, listen, and pause long enough to appreciate what we have.

As I mentioned earlier, my son Danny was profoundly retarded because of his disability, Hunter's Syndrome. When he was four or five, I took him to the beautiful lagoon by Lake Michigan, near our home. I used to drive past there every day on my way to the university, my mind filled with busy thoughts. I didn't really see the lagoon or its charming residents. Danny got out of the car and saw the array of mallard ducks with their stunningly-colored wings. He grabbed my leg and shouted: "Look, Daddy, look!" When Danny died a few years later, I put that moment into his eulogy. I saw it as Danny's valedictory to an unmindful and ungrateful world. "Look! For goodness sake, look!" Danny begs us. Pause long enough to be stunned at the budding of the rose, the setting of the sun, the smile of the infant, the wagging tail of the dog. This little boy with blighted mind but exquisite *mindfulness* saw more than "normal" people do. Danny was retarded, but he was not blasé. We are blasé—damnably so. The goodness of life escapes us. We attend more to what we want than to what we have. Buddhism wants us to cool the rat race and leave time for ecstasy. And Buddhism never gives up on the hope that we can be changed.

Ecologist Annie Dillard gives us a useful exercise in mindfulness. She bids us look at that stuff we call dirt, or better, topsoil. A square foot tray of topsoil one inch deep is a miracle of life and vitality. It contains "an average of 1,356 living creatures, . . . including 865 mites, 265 springtails, 22 millipedes, 19 adult beetles, plus various numbers of 12 other life forms." On top of that are two billion bacteria and millions of fungi, protozoans, and algae. We should kneel in the presence of topsoil. Our lives depend on it. It takes millennia to form. It is just one of the earth miracles of which we are not mindful. Slow down, says Buddhism, and look around.

So there it is, a little primer on Buddhism, a peek into the heart of this spirituality. Before getting into the nitty-gritty of Buddhist attitudes on contraception and abortion, we can see from the above an ethic friendly to family planning and to ecological concerns. Buddhism eschews excess—too much consuming, too much reproducing, too much unnecessary harm to our parent Earth and its privileged residents.

Buddhism and Contraception

Parichart Suwanbubbha, a professor at Mahidol University in Bangkok, Thailand, will be our principal guide to how Buddhism tackles the ethics of contraception and abortion. Suwanbubbha concedes that much of Buddhism is *pronatalist*, that is, in favor of reproduction. After all, in Buddhist thought, only human beings are able to attain *Nirvana*. Making lots of them would therefore seem to be, as Suwanbubbha says, "a good sign of a general improvement in the moral state of the universe."

A lot of life experience informs the Buddhist tradition, however, and Buddhism is open to family planning and contraception. In Suwanbubbha's words, "it is possible to say that Buddhist teachings allow individuals, including women, to have the right to plan their family according to their own circumstances using any methods of safe contraception." The *Middle Way* supports this, since there can be too many children. Also, "economic misery and quality of life of all members in a family" can justify contraception. The Buddha taught that poverty can become the cause of crimes, a view also held by Aristotle and Thomas Aquinas, as we saw in chapter 1. Inasmuch as this relates to "an excessive birth rate," family planning should be allowed; and good government, in Buddhist thinking, should provide the services for those who want them. William

LaFleur says that for Buddhists in Asia "there is absolutely nothing wrong with preventing conception." It is an
obvious application of the Middle Way.

The result of this teaching in Thailand shows in the fertility rate. It stands just below the replacement level, at 1.9
births per woman. The contraceptive rate for married
women of reproductive age is 72.2 percent. This shows
that Buddhism does not discourage contraception for fam
ily planning. The abortion question, however, involves
more agonizing. To that we turn next.

Buddhists and Abortion

Most Buddhists believe in reincarnation. This relates
directly to Buddhist views of abortion. Buddhism believes
that life begins at the time of conception when three conditions combine: (1) the father and mother have sexual
intercourse; (2) it is the mother's fertile period; and (3)
there is a "being to be born" (gandhabba) present, ready
to reenter life in the form of a baby. This would seem to
block any permission of abortion, since in this view, the
fetus would seem to have rights equal to that of adults.
"Right Action," one of the rules of the Eight-fold Path,
forbids killing. It says: "I will not willingly take the life of
a living thing." That includes animals as well as fetuses,
and this is called the *First Precept of Buddhism*. An early
Buddhist text said: "As far as the human being is concerned, even the abortion of an embryo which was just
conceived is regarded as a crime." So there goes any right
to abortion. On top of that, as Suwanbubbha says, "the
act of killing will certainly produce retribution" by way of
the doctrine of *karma*. Part of the retribution could be
seriously nasty—the shortening of your life, or a continu-
ing tendency to disease if you were involved in performing
the abortion.

So the immediate conclusion would seem to be that Buddhism absolutely forbids abortion. The operative word here is *seem*. As we saw in Hinduism, however, the prohibition against killing comes on like an absolute, but then it runs into life with all of its complexity, and exceptions and accommodations are made. Aquinas said that life is marked by *quasi infinitae diversitates,* an infinity of variations. Religions and their moral systems that endure notice this and adapt to it. Christianity adapts, for example. Christians have a commandment that tells them not to kill. Then they go on to interpret it to mean that murder is what is always wrong, but not every homicide is murder. Things like capital punishment and war have been justified by many Christians, Jews, and Muslims. Jesus was pretty clear in saying that his followers should sell all they have and give it to the poor, but few are the Christians who haven't found a way out of that demand. Christian scholars say it is a "counsel," not a "precept or a commandment." All this may seem like quibbling, but it may also be seen as coping successfully with the facts of a life in which ideals cannot always be realized.

These ancient systems of thought liked to proclaim the ideal—and not killing is plainly the ideal—and to proclaim it as an absolute law or commandment. Then they discover that absolutes do not play out well in real life. This is exactly what happened in Buddhism. After saying that no killing is the first precept of Buddhist life, they honor life by making the exceptions it requires. Phra Depvethee, a Thai Buddhist monk, says that all beings are not equal. Some have higher standing. For example, you could not kill a mother to save a fetus, because the mother is a more developed person and can contribute many important and valuable things to her family and society. As Parichart says, "if there is only one choice, the mother's life should be saved, not the fetus." You could, in other words, abort the fetus to save the mother, but you could not endanger the mother to save the fetus.

Unlessment

As always happens in ethics, the *unlessment* door opens. Thou shalt not kill—*unless*. So, in Buddhism, you can kill a fetus if it is necessary to save a mother. Also, Suwanbubbha says, it is right for physicians to abort fetuses if their mothers have HIV infections. "This would be considered a good intention and a good means for a mercy killing of fetuses, even though these cases are illegal in Thailand." This would be acceptable to many Buddhists, "since the medical personnel do not perform such actions owing to greed, hate, or delusion." As she says, all Buddhists might not agree on this; as in all other religions, there are few things on which all agree. Yet this is a respectable Buddhist position.

And there is more. We saw that *karma* enters into abortion decisions. Abortion is a decision that results in the death of a fetus. That leaves those who perform it open to bad *karma*. But you can change your *karma*. Here is the way Buddhists explain it : "According to Buddhism, when one *karma* is still bearing its fruit, other *karma* with the same or lesser potency do not have the chance to ripen. Only when the *karma* currently bearing fruit is weak or exhausted can other *karma* have an opportunity to replace it." This means, Suwanbubbha says, that performing good deeds can build up so much good *karma* that it simply overwhelms the bad *karma* resulting from an abortion. The bad *karma* can become "lapsed *karma*." It is simply superseded, and you are, as it were, home free.

Furthermore, the Buddha made an exception for an offense performed by one who "has carefully cultured body, habits, and thought: He has developed insight." Insight—enlightenment to Buddhists—means goodness and virtue. When such a good person performs an offense, less bad *karma* results. Good persons have enormous stores of good *karma*. An offense by them could be considered, Suwanbubbha says, "like throwing a grain of salt into the river Ganges. Due to the mass of water in the big river, the water would not become salty and undrinkable." When a morally bad person performs an offense, it "is like throwing a grain of salt into a little cup of water: The water would become salty and undrinkable because of a little quantity of water in the cup." She continues, "the bad action of a good person is insignificant compared to his or her accumulated good actions." A good woman who has an abortion, may, by this doctrine, "feel relief, hope, and encouragement." In effect, the abortion may become what Catholics would call a *venial sin*, a forgivable sin, unlike the seriousness of a *mortal sin*. But even mortal sins can be forgiven in Catholic teaching.

Intention is also central in Buddhist morality. The motive for an abortion affects its morality. An abortion performed for good motives, says Suwanbubbha, uncontaminated by greed, hatred, anger, or delusion, will not be considered as serious a moral issue. The bad *karma* that might result would be greatly limited by the compassionate intentions. An abortion done out of self-indulgence is more serious. Buddhists would not justify an abortion done for purposes of sex selection, since wanting only one gender would imply hatred of the other. That would poison the intention. Also, wisdom (*panna*) is an important moral criterion. So, says Suwanbubbha, "Buddhist criteria for the ethics of abortion are open to using wisdom" to see if the motive for the abortion is marked by compassion and not by any negative emotion.

Suwanbubbha argues with other Buddhist scholars that the right to abortion should be expanded in Buddhist countries such as Thailand. She asks: "Why don't we expand the definition of the threat to the mother's life in Thai law to cover more necessary reasons of the present situation, such as contraceptive failure and economic hardship in accordance with Buddhist norms based on 'wholesome intention' and 'wholesome consequences'?" She adds, "This would be a good way to help both suffering pregnant women, and at the same time it is not obviously contrasting to Buddhist teachings." A Buddhist woman can have an abortion and still be a good Buddhist. Suwanbubbha concludes that Buddhism allows "enough freedom to choose the way. Whatever one decides, one has to be brave enough to accept the consequences." As always, compassion has the last word in Buddhism.

When all of these considerations are applied to abortion, it does not mean that abortion is nothing or morally neutral. It would still be better if no abortions were needed, but Buddhism, like the other religions studied in this book, faces the fact that abortion may sometimes be the best decision and a truly moral choice.

[margin note: good summary statement]

Japanese Buddhism

William LaFleur, professor of Japanese studies, is the author of *Liquid Life: Abortion and Buddhism in Japan.* He shows in this remarkable study how a contemporary Japanese woman could accept Buddhism with its First Precept against killing, have an abortion, and still consider herself a Buddhist in good standing.

Japanese Buddhists have a long experience with family planning, including abortion. In fact, population growth stopped from 1721 to 1846. It had been climbing rapidly. Suddenly it stopped, and population leveled. There was no government effort to stem growth. On the contrary, the government wanted increased growth; they thought it would strengthen Japan. Thomas Malthus had famously said that what stops population growth are the terrible three: war, famine, and epidemic. There is no evidence, however, that these factors were sufficiently present to explain the stabilization of Japan's population. LaFleur concludes that the "decisions about having fewer children than had once been the custom were being made within the 'bedrooms' of the Japanese citizenry." Their main method of limiting births? LaFleur and other scholars say "infanticide and abortion" were widely used.

Does this mean that Japanese Buddhists were cold-hearted and cruel, and should we invoke the old saw that Asians see life as "cheap"? If we do that, we should first remember what we saw in chapter 3 about the widespread use of infanticide and abandonment in medieval Christian Europe when people had little access to reliable contraception or safe surgical abortion. Also, there is no evidence that Japan was deficient in family values. When Francis Xavier (1506–52) visited Japan, he remarked: "Judging by the people we have so far met, I would say that the Japanese are the best race yet discovered and I do not think you will find their match among the pagan nations." As LaFleur says: "This is, to say the least, rather high praise for the moral tenor of a society that, exactly at that time, countenanced both abortion and infanticide."

Japan has always strongly valued children. François Caron, who lived in Japan in the early seventeenth century, made this observation: "Children are carefully and tenderly brought up; their parents strike them seldom or never, and though they cry whole nights together, they endeavor to still them with patience; judging that infants have no understanding, but that it grows with them as they grow in years, and therefore they are to be encouraged with indulgences and examples."

LaFleur sees all of this as "evidence that there is no necessary correlation between the allowance of abortion and the quality—or even the overall tenor—of family life in a given society . . . Apparently it is possible for a society to practice abortion and still have what is generally called a 'strong' conception of the family." Additional proof may be found inversely in those modern right-wing resisters to abortion rights who, with all their talk of *family values*, display no great concern for born children, their schools, their families, or their welfare. There are lessons here. Do not equate the use of abortion with cruelty or resistance to it with gentleness. It's just not that simple.

Learning from Rituals

How did Japanese Buddhists decide abortion was compatible with their gentle religion? The answer is found not so much in texts, as we Westerners would want, as in rituals and symbols. Because the symbols and the rituals surrounding them are unfamiliar to us, we could easily scorn them. That would be a mistake. We should never belittle the ways in which people deal with pain. Even today, we can see that Japanese Buddhists do not take abortions lightly. They do not forget the aborted fetus, which they see, in LaFleur's words "not so much as being 'terminated' as being put on 'hold,' asked to bide its time in some other world." Remember the doctrine of reincarnation that is common in Buddhism. A being was going to be born. For reasons judged good by the would-be parents, that birthing was stopped, but the being who would be born is put back in waiting. The "life" that was rejected or that died through miscarriage or early infant death is called a *mizuko,* and parents pray for its well-being in the sacred

realms to which it has been "returned." Elaborate rituals
are employed to remember these rejected "lives." Little
child-size statues of Jizo, a sweet savior-figure associated
closely with children, are found in abundance and are visited by parents who lost children or had abortions. In
some images, Jizo wraps the *mizukos* under his protective
cape and gives them comfort. In a time when infant mortality was high, as LaFleur says, "the idea that such children were being pulled back into a basically 'good' world
of the gods and Buddhas to some extent palliated parental
pain." There is nothing coldhearted about the care of the
mizuko. And it is not dissimilar to my mother's belief that
the many children she saw die in old Ireland were being
taken to heaven by God as angels to pray for their surviving families.

In much of Buddhism, birth is seen as a gradual
process, not a moment. Progress was celebrated, but it
was not until age fifteen—or age twenty today—that the
child was considered a full human. Prior to that, the child
was slowly moving out of the sacred realm of the Buddhas. Returning them to that realm through abortion was
not the same as killing an adult, especially since they had
a chance to return in better circumstances or even to enter
Nirvana. Many Christian leaders in the early centuries
rejected any such gradualism and decided that the "image
of God" was stamped on the earliest embryonic manifestations of life. Even male masturbation was called homicide.
Potential life was simply stipulated to have full personal
status. The yellow flower on the tomato plant was to be
treated as a tomato. Common sense is offended by such
thinking, and sensible debate on abortion is short-circuited.

A final thought on Buddhism: Buddhism, overall, has
accepted sexuality as a good; it also appreciates the use of
non-procreative sex for the sheer joy of it. Christianity

could learn from this. James Brundage, in his *Law, Sex and Christian Society in Medieval Europe,* refers to "the Christian horror of sex." Sex was even seen as the cause of the "original sin" that fouled the souls of newborns till baptism cleansed them. Such a view is an invitation to neurosis. It is not essential to Christian teaching, and it made a realistic discussion of abortion difficult. Reproduction came to be seen as the only justification for sex, since sex was seen as morally sordid. Sexual thoughts are still called "dirty" in much of the West. East and West have much to learn from one another. That conviction is the soul of this book.

6. Chinese Religious Wisdom

EURO-AMERICAN PRIDE IS A PROBLEM when we look at the more ancient—and thus more experienced—cultures of the East. We white Euro-Americans really do believe we are the master race. The fact that we are a dwindling minority on the planet and Johnny-come-latelies to civilization is something we would be wise to remember. Long before we came on the scene and ages before our Jewish, Christian, and Islamic religions were formed, the ancient Chinese were highly sophisticated philosophically and even scientifically. Some of the religious insights we explore in this chapter can be traced back over four thousand years. The Chinese made the first seismograph when Jesus was still alive, and they were systematically charting spots on the sun a generation before Jesus was born. There was smallpox inoculation in China as early as the eleventh century; the inoculation was not introduced into Europe until the eighteenth century.

The theories of these bright people are worth a hearing. All theory is a distillation of experience. Experience is the best teacher, as the saying goes, and the Chinese have had a lot of it. A visit to their wisdom is worth the effort.

Our first guide is Geling Shang, currently at the Harvard-Yenching Institute at Harvard University. Shang has studied the religions of China, particularly Taoism and Confucianism. He insists that you cannot understand the history or culture of China, even during its Communist period, without understanding its religions. For example, Shang refers to "the notorious effectiveness of China's campaign of family planning and its "one child" policy, initiated by the Communist government and supported by Marxist ideology. As to its effectiveness, historian Paul Kennedy reports on scholarly estimates that 240 million more Chinese would have been born over the two decades when this policy was being enforced. The drop in fertility rate from six children per woman before 1970 to near replacement level in 1990 was the fastest decline ever reported in any country, and some scholars attribute half of this decline to government policies. So there is reason to say it was effective. More puzzling, Shang says, at least for Western observers, is why there was so much acceptance of the policy by the Chinese people.

Westerners, he says, can understandably ask: "Why does this campaign not meet much resistance from the majority of Chinese people, though it is seen as manifestly coercive and even violent when measured by the Western standards of human rights?" Of course, most in the West believe that it was not supported by the people but simply forced on them by the Communist regime, but that is inaccurate. There was, indeed, resistance to some of its more drastic manifestations, but overall, there was acceptance of the policy. Comparative religion scholars Jordan and Li Chuang Paper say: "The policy could not have continued for this length of time and been moderately successful were the people not, to a large degree, supporting it." They add another corrective to much Western thinking: "China is not the highly centralized totalitarian state depicted in the Western press. Regional governments can and do ignore central directives, and the police, usually unarmed, can only enforce laws which are supported by the population, for to do otherwise can lead to being beaten by the populace."

The way the Chinese prefer to bring about change, the Papers say, is through education and moral persuasion.

Some of the compliance with this stern policy was motivated by simple practicality. People notice when there are too many people. As Luo Ping, sociologist and director of the Women's Studies Center at Wuhan University observes: "Family planning must be implemented in a country like China where the size of the population puts too much pressure on the economy and on society. . . . China is just like a small boat which can only carry 100 people but already has 110 in it."

Actually, the "one child" policy was intended as a temporary emergency measure and is now being phased out, according to the Population Institute. "It was only meant to influence one generation," said Li Cheng Sheng, director of China's State Family Planning Commission. "If this generation had fewer children, it would slow population growth and solve the problem. But if we continue to carry it out, it would make for a bad family structure."

A Culture Shaped by Religion

Shang, however, says that none of the above is understandable without taking religion into account. Chinese culture, which has been defined and shaped by Chinese religion for over four thousand years, was a "spiritual resource which has enabled Chinese people to tolerate, accept, and even support the modern idea of family planning." The Chinese religions that Shang refers to are Taoism (usually pronounced *dowism*) and Confucianism, which are the principal religions in China (though not the only religions). (Buddhism is also present in China.) Taoism and Confucianism vary in many ways, but they also share some understandings of reality. They agree on this one central position: "*Peace and harmony* are the ultimate state of the whole universe and the ultimate goal of human life." All policies and all individual lives must be geared to peace and harmony. When this goal is met, "the whole universe with its 'ten thousand beings' flourishes, pros-pers, and celebrates," says Shang.

To enter the world of Chinese religion, we must be introduced to some of its basic concepts, and we can add a few Chinese words to our vocabulary. Remember, words are windows into the soul. We are peering into the soul of an ancient and sophisticated culture in which people like us rose to the same sun and ended their individual days under the same moon. We are entering into the living room of their culture, and when we do such a thing, we should tread lightly, with eyes and ears wide open to see what they have made of it all. Here we will meet new terms such as *Tao, Mandate of Heaven, ch'i,* and *jen.*

Religion without God

When we in the Western world think of religion, we are influenced mainly by Judaism, Christianity, and Islam. These religions are theistic to the core, that is, they all believe in a personal God. It is hard for Westerners to think of religion in any other way. If, however, we want to be open to other cultures and their wisdom, we must try to see the different conclusions other good people came up with as they tried to make sense of the universe. As pro-fessor of Chinese studies Chun Fang Yu tells us: "Unlike most other religions, Chinese religion does not have a cre-ator God. There is no God transcendent and separate from the world and there is no heaven outside of the universe to which human beings would want to go for refuge." That's a shocker to most people in our part of the world, but let's see where this kind of thinking led the Chinese. Unlike the Jewish scriptures that start their origins story with "In the beginning . . . " there is no beginning of the universe for the Chinese. It always was.

The universe, "Heaven and Earth," as they say, "is the origin of everything including human beings," Yu tells us.

There is a creating and sustaining force in the universe called the *Tao,* which means "the way." The Tao, which is like the Western "natural law " and the Hindu *Dharma,* points the way toward harmony. Conforming to the Tao is our moral duty. This is called the *Mandate of Heaven.* When we don't obey the Mandate of Heaven, which urges us toward self-restraint, humility, and unselfishness, confusion and destruction follow. Rulers have to follow the Mandate of Heaven, or they lose their right to rule.

This is not the heaven of Christians, a place where God and the blessed reside. In the Christian and Islamic view, as Daniel Overmyer puts it, "it is really God that is sacred, not the world itself." In the Chinese perspective, however, sacredness is a quality of the universe, and the Mandate of Heaven is a mandate of that sacred universe of which we are a part. Overmyer says, "this view of the world is similar to that of many other cultures, such as the Hopi or the Sioux in North America, but it is different from the traditional teachings of Judaism, Christianity, and Islam." Another basic aspect of this worldview is the concept of *yin* and *yang.*

Yin and Yang

Reality, the ancient Chinese concluded, is full of polarities such as day and night, bitter and sweet, winter and summer, male and female. They called this natural harmony of opposites *yin* and *yang.* That is why everything, including meals (we notice this in Chinese cooking) should be in conformity with this bipolarity, balancing sour and sweet, peppery and bland. This reality of which we are born, with its *yin* and its *yang,* is a reality in which everything and everybody are made of the same material. They call this material *ch'i.* Ch'i is the basic reality of all that is, including the rocks, the lilies, and us! National boundaries would mean nothing, because reality is shared being. We are all made of the same basic stuff. Damaging nature would make no sense. Nature and humans are all part of the same miracle.

This reality, this world, in which everything is made of the same stuff, deserves our fullest respect. And here is our final Chinese word; the word for that respect is *jen,* the greatest of the virtues according to Confucius. *Jen* implies a largeness of heart, sincerity, compassion, and a sense of our relationship to all that is in the universe. It is the essence of true humanity. To have it is to be a truly humane person. Not to have it is to court disaster.

All of this appears in an "inscription" that is seen as a Confucian creed. It goes like this:

> Heaven is my father and Earth is my mother, and even such a small creature as I find an intimate place in their midst. Therefore that which fills the universe I regard as my body and that which directs the universe I consider as my nature. All people are my brothers and sisters, and all things are my companions. The great ruler (the emperor) is the eldest son of my parents (Heaven and Earth), and the great ministers are his stewards. Respect the ages—that is the way to treat them. Show deep love toward the orphaned and the weak—this is the way to treat them. The sage identifies his character with that of Heaven and Earth. Even those who are tired, infirm, crippled, or sick; those who have no brothers or children, wives or husbands, are all my brothers and sisters who are in distress and have no one to turn to. In life I honor and serve Heaven and Earth. In death I will be at peace.

In that list of virtues, Jews, Christians, and Muslims will hear the voices of Isaiah, Jesus, and the prophet Mohammed urging us to have compassion on the orphans, the widows, and the poor. Compassion is the DNA of all great religions. These things we must do, the Chinese say.

We must be people of *jen*, following the Tao. It is the Mandate of Heaven. Thwarting the mandate means trouble. If life is a mess, it's a mess of our making. One Chinese saying puts it this way: "Curses and blessing do not come though the door uninvited. Human beings invite their arrival. The reward of good and evil is like the shadow accompanying a body, and so it is apparent that heaven and earth are possessed of crime-recording spirits." (Again we see similarities to the doctrines of *dharma* and *karma* from Hinduism and Buddhism.) We can't hide from reckless or self-indulgent living. We have to plan and think about the results of our behavior on our mother, the Earth. The effects of our deeds follow us like a shadow follows the body. Heaven and Earth keep records; they record our crimes and punish us for them. This ancient teaching contains a lot of realism. If anything, it is more relevant today than it ever was, now that our capacity to destroy exceeds the earth's capacity to heal. A humanity filled with *jen* and reverence for the Mandate of Heaven would make this earth a garden. The alternative is to make it a garbage heap. And we will pay the price in disease and pain and hunger. Our shadows follow us.

Now let us return to Shang's guidance and see how this applies to family planning.

Family Planning in Chinese Religions

Shang tells us that the Chinese have been involved in family planning for thousands of years, perhaps longer than any people on record. Undergirding their interest "is the Chinese concept of universal harmony, a moral ideal and religious belief" shared by Confucianism, Taoism, and Chinese Buddhism. The Chinese and all their religious traditions have believed "that the human phenomena of reproduction, sexuality and family life could gravely affect the balance, order and harmony of human society and the natural world." Shang says: "Chinese people have become accustomed to thinking, under the influence of these traditions, that the way we act and the things we have done even in everyday life might affect the state of our family, community, nation and the whole world." Their concern for family planning was never a private matter, as in much of the individualistic West. It was a matter of social obligation to have more or fewer children as demanded by the common good. In Shang's words: "In Chinese traditions there is very little room for individuals or private rights apart from the roles and duties one is to fulfill."

You could say their approach was based on family values, but it was a different concept of family values, unlike the one touted by modern United States conservatives. The family was the basic unit of society. As Shang says, "before any individual and before society, there is the family." Family in China became the archetype, the model of all social reality. Even society was seen as a family writ large. The nation has been called "a nation-family." There are important moral implications to this. If the whole nation, and by extension the whole human race, is a family, then we are concerned for the good of all. There are no outsiders. Indeed, this broader Chinese notion of family includes not only the living but also the dead, and even the future unborn. It is expansive, not inbred. Too often, the Western "family" is an occluded, egotistical island. Not so in China, and that adds richness to their culture.

Interestingly, this idea of family matches one of the central ideas in Judaism, Christianity, and Islam. The Hebrew Bible saw the household or the family as the model for society. Creation in this perspective is God's household, and as Christian theologian Douglas Meeks says, the first and last question of economics from the biblical perspective is: "Will everyone in the household get what it takes to live?" You don't leave people out or ignore them in a family.

It is like the cartoon that showed a mother and father and three children seated at the kitchen table, with bills all over the table. The father announces gravely: "Because of inflationary pressures, I'm going to have to let two of you go!" It's a funny cartoon because that is not the way it happens in a family. In times of stress, we find new ways of sharing; we don't discard a couple of the children. Corporations in the East used to think of themselves as a family and did not fire people. If people could not keep up with the pace of one job, they would train them for something else. Unfortunately, a crueler Western approach is seeping into these corporations, and letting people go has become the norm.

A nation that thought of itself as a family would share generously and would always be thinking socially. We would not just think of our "own" family as the center of the universe. Chinese culture was imbued with a strong social conscience, and this was reinforced by its religions. It shows up in its approach to family planning, in the readiness of the Chinese to cooperate with the government when more people were needed and also when fewer people were the requirement.

Too Many, Too Few

Like all the ancient religions, Confucianism was born in a world in which life was short and perilous. Fertility was stressed. The Confucian writer Mencius said: "There are three things which are unfilial, and to have no posterity is the worst of them." Shang says: "Many Chinese, if not most, still believe in this today." Through history, Chinese leaders stressed the need to expand the population.

Confucius himself said: "A noble man would be ashamed of land waste due to a lack of people." Duke Yue ruled that if a twenty-year-old man or a seventeen-year-old woman were unmarried, the parents would be charged as criminals. Rewards were given for having a baby—two gallons of wine and a dog for a son and two gallons of wine and a baby pig for a daughter. A welfare system also supported the children. When you had two children, the government supplied additional food and nursing care if needed. If the parents were ill or died, "the government would look after their children," Shang tells us. The government was involved because fear of having too few people was an issue for "the nation-family."

Shang tells us that Taoism, however, was an interesting exception to this ancient stress on fertility. Their ideal society was "the small state with a little population" that could prevent people from battling for land, food, and other resources. This view shows up in later jurists, who argued that population should be controlled according to the needs of the state.

When the early Communist government in China urged people to reproduce, they did; when that government realized that overpopulation was the new threat, the people cooperated with the new need to limit births. The reasoning was the same: There will be no harmony and balance in the world if the number of people outstrips the land's resources. Remember, in their view, we, the water, the topsoil, and the rest of nature are made of the same stuff, and we must live in harmony. The universe is a community, and everybody and everything have to get along.

Other things in the Chinese religious culture helped the modern family planning effort. The ancient traditions always stressed the *quality* of offspring, not the *quantity*. People should not marry or reproduce too soon. The very young might not be ready to parent healthy children. Some even held that men should be thirty years old and women twenty before marrying, since before that time they are not physically and mentally mature enough to produce healthy and well-developed children. As Shang says, "there is a right season for growing crops, and there is a right time for marriage." Sometimes premature marriage was forbidden by law, and "those who violated such laws would be fined or heavily taxed by the government." The Communist "one child" policy had a family planning history to build on.

The belief that sex is good is another helpful aspect of Chinese culture. One of the weaknesses in Christian history was the belief that sex is bad, and only reproduction validates it. Sex was a valued gift in China, aside from its capacity to make babies. Sex was utterly natural, the primary example of *yin* and *yang*. One of the purposes of sex was reproduction, but pleasure and health are on an equal plane. Sex is good for you, and the Chinese religions celebrated what Shang calls "the joy of sexual interplay." The Taoists, in fact, unlike the Confucians, put more emphasis on the joy and healthfulness of sex than they did on reproduction. A good sex life—marked by both pleasure and restraint—was the secret of longevity. The Taoists developed, as we shall see, "the art of the bed chamber" to maximize the pleasure and delights of a good sex life for both men and women. They knew that there is a lot more to sex than making babies. How right they were—in real life, sex is rarely used for the purpose of making a baby.

But What about Abortion?

Abortion is always a thorny issue, an unfortunate necessity at best. How did the Chinese handle it? One thing is certain, says Shang: "The Chinese have employed abortion

for various purposes since ancient times." There was "no
explicit code" to prohibit it. At the same time, it was
viewed as "unfavorable" and "was carried out by midwives rather than official physicians." It was seen as a private matter, needed to handle a private crisis. In spite of its
"unfavorable" rating, Shang tells us, "Chinese attitudes
toward abortion were mostly tolerant and compassionate.
People did not think it was wrong unless it was done
unnecessarily."

An important ethics text was called the "Table of Merits and Errors." The Table tried to quantify the wrongness
of various activities—again, something like the Catholic
division into mortal and venial (forgivable) sins. So abortion was considered a 300-point error, which was 200
points less than setting fire to someone's house. It was the
same kind of error as inducing someone to gamble, but it
was not even close to the murder of a person, which was a
1,000-point crime!

Abortion was clearly part of the "one child" policy of
the Chinese government. How did that fit in with Chinese
religion and culture? Shang says that "the Chinese religions have always prioritized social values over the concerns of the individual. Where conflict arose between
society and individuals, the latter were expected to sacrifice their needs to serve the common good. If abortion
profits the family or society, then it is reasonable to do it.
Even an adult is supposed to be ready to sacrifice his life
for the family and society, so why not a fetus?" Of course
there was appropriate criticism in and outside of China of
the "poor medical conditions of abortions that take place
in China, or the forceful aggressiveness of some local offi-
cers in enforcing the policy." Still, Shang says, abortion
"has never been a religious issue for Chinese."

It was viewed, sensibly, as a sometime necessity. Those who are dogmatically opposed to all abortions must realize that most people and most cultures do not agree with them.

As in Christianity, Buddhism, and Hinduism, infanticide and abandonment were practiced by the ancient Chinese, usually as a result of poverty and famine. Female babies were the prime victims of these practices. There was moral resistance to this. The Table of Merits and Errors counted infanticide as a 1,000-point error, the same as for the murder of an adult.

In conclusion, then, the religions of China have long considered family planning a necessity. It is based on the need for universal harmony rather than on Communist ideology or other Western influences. Contraception, even abortion when needed, are accepted in this ancient moral tradition.

not well discussed

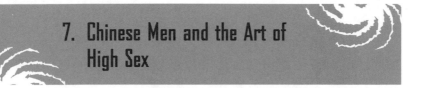

7. Chinese Men and the Art of High Sex

POPE PIUS XII, IN HIS WEEKLY AUDIENCE WITH TOURISTS, often opened with the line: "He who travels far, learns much." In this book, we are traveling far to see what other people have thought of the life we all live. Every religion develops stories to explain reality and shape a view of the world that makes sense. None of these religions is fully successful. In modern public relations terms, each religion puts a spin on reality. If we only know the religion that dominates in our culture and its spin on reality, we are limited, locked in a cocoon. Our sense of reality is impaired, because we have only seen one version of it. We have already toured some of the religions that were spawned in the Near East and the Orient. From there, they spread around the world, learning from experience and changing and adapting as all religions do. Our particular focus is on how they dealt with sex, gender relations, and reproduction.

In this chapter, our principal guide is Hsiung Ping-chen of the Academia Sinica in Taipei, Taiwan. Throughout her career, Hsiung has studied the rich history of her people. She joined our project to share some of the special attitudes the Chinese had regarding sex, and particularly how they dealt with men. The Chinese realized early on that when it comes to sex, men are a bit of a problem.

Hsiung is not unkind to men. She says that male sexuality has been caricatured in nasty ways in both modern and ancient times. Males are presented as reckless studs "driven by endless carnal desires, always ready to indulge and hardly capable of constraint." They are widely seen as uninterested "in limiting the number of children or disciplining their sexual drives."

The long history of China shows that it is not that simple. Of course, the Chinese knew that men were not low on sexual energy and were not bashful about pursuing their sexual goals. Their cultures and their religions addressed that fact of life. The Chinese did not allow sex or family planning to be classified as *women's work*. They acknowledged that in their history—as in most societies— males were largely in charge. Religious and political authority was in their grasp. Therefore, when it comes to something as important for "universal harmony" as sexuality and reproduction, we had better deal with the guys.

The Chinese knew that sex is powerful. It can purr like a kitten, but it has the strength of a tiger. We can either control it, or it can chaotically control us. Still, as Hsiung says, sexuality in the Chinese religious traditions of Taoism, Confucianism, and Buddhism did not have "the overall shadowing of a puritanical association of human sex with guilt, sin, or shame." Sex was good and delightful, and it was to be appreciated and regulated. Special efforts were made to remind males of this.

The Magnificent Pleasure of High Sex

Hsiung uses the suggestive term "high sex" to show the first lesson from Chinese culture. Sex is not an inconsequential pleasure of the grab-it-when-you-can variety. Proper sex is high art, an exercise in sensitivity and delicacy. It has many purposes. For years, Christians taught that the primary purpose for sex is reproduction, and all other purposes are secondary. The Chinese disagree. Reproduction is one purpose of heterosexual sex, but not the usual or the primary. Sex had four equally important purposes:

spiritual elevation, the promotion of health, successful reproduction, and *personal pleasure.* Proper sex in the right time, place, and circumstance promoted longevity and spiritual depth. Obviously, in this worldview, thoughts of such sex are not *dirty,* nor are joyful jokes about such sex *dirty jokes.*

Taoism was particularly keen on enhancing the joys and pleasures of sex. Taoists wrote extensively on "the art of the bed chamber." High sex is not just tumbled into; it was the product of care and a healthy life style. It is said that President John F. Kennedy got the United States into exercise in a big way for the first time. The Chinese were far ahead on this. For a healthy sexual life, we should feed ourselves well, sleep well, and exercise. Sex is one of the most natural of the world's forces, and we should view it with respect. Modern science has confirmed what these people knew millennia ago: Poor nutrition and lack of exercise can decrease sexual potential—including male potency. Men should realize their responsibility for the success of sex. Men were instructed in the skills of pleasing a woman. Good sex requires *jen,* respect, and concern for the other. Men should bring a kind of "nurturing kindness" into their lovemaking and become connoisseurs of "achieving the magnificent pleasure for both women and men." For sex to be good, Hsiung tells us, "the emotional and physical gratification of both the male and the female parties is essential, as the deficiency in either compromises the desired effects."

Part of the high art of lovemaking involves giving attention to the right moment—what was called "the heavenly moment." The best time for a man to make love to a woman is when she shows "a desire to engage that is almost unsuppressible." Don't assume your partner is ready when you are. Love is patient and sweetly opportunistic. Some things are detrimental to good sex: exhaustion, anger, too much to drink, overeating, and not enough exercise. Poorly done sex could also have adverse effects on reproduction. Bad effects, Hsiung tells us, were seen as related to "whether one was to beget any offspring, whether a boy might be hoped for, and whether the child one received would live to maturity, and turn out to be smart and capable." Some of the details for preparing and doing sex well were referred to as *Tao,* the term for spiritual and moral rectitude from which Taoism takes its name. Again, this stresses the spiritual significance of sex done well. Rather than being dirty, sexual pleasure has a kind of sacramental value.

The Chinese, however, did conclude that in sex, as in the rest of life, it was possible to have too much of a good thing. Taoists strongly believed in what Hsiung calls "a 'zero sum' nature of the reserve of male essence (semen)." There was, in this view, only so much that a man had to offer, and if he had too much sex, the quality of it for reproduction and pleasure could decrease. To some degree, this had in it a bit of the old French adage that pleasure delayed is pleasure increased. They were also concerned with producing healthy offspring who would be loyal. Men feared, in Hsiung's words, "that their overused male organ could fail them in the task of successful coital performance and in successful reproduction. . . . Anxieties over the premature depletion of the male essence and an inadequate supply of 'kidney water' (the source of male sexuality) was a constant factor in Chinese giddy gossips and popular medical advertisements." Overindulgence would lead to too much extraction of the limited supply of male sperm. There was even a lot of discussion about the advisability of coitus interruptus. Underlying all this, Hsiung says, may have been the insight that "self-restraint in sex is probably a useful and necessary habit." Whatever the intentions behind the idea that male sperm was limited, it would certainly have had the effect of taming male sexual impetuosity. It also taught that quality was more important than quantity in sex. Better infrequent high sex than frequent low and careless sex.

Sleeping Alone

Praising celibacy rose out of the idea that you could over-do sex. "Songs of Sleeping Alone" were widespread, especially as people aged, and especially for men. It appealed because celibacy conserved your overall energy and gave you a healthier old age. Hsiung tells of a particularly "bouncy man name Pao Hui," who lived in the twelfth century. Minister Chia Ss'u-tao observed the elderly Pao "getting up and down the stairs, bowing and kneeling at this and that altar with little difficulty." He wanted to know Pao's secret to having such a long healthy life. Pao replied that his "technique of maintenance and nourishment had to do with a kind of special 'pill' he took from an unspeakable source." Chia wanted the recipe. At this point, Pao smiled and disclosed his secret prescription: "What your humble servant has been taking for fifty years is the pill of sleeping alone."

As in any tradition, consensus is hard to come by, especially in something as intimate and personal as sex. As we would imagine, there were vigorous oldsters who wanted not just to run up stairs nimbly but also to enjoy their vigor in bed. The much admired eighteenth-century poet Yuan Mei confessed that "for the better half of my life I never slept by myself unless lying down in illness." Others said that resisting sex all the time would take more energy than it would give you. They asked: "What benefit was left after every ounce of energy and bit of spirit one had were spent suppressing the desire for sexual union?"

Chinese "Viagra"

Since sex was a positive good and a path to health and spiritual growth, the Chinese were concerned about sexual health and the ability to have sex. The problem of male impotence received much attention. The pharmaceutical texts of Yueh attended to it in great detail. To enhance male potency and for "fruitful sex," Yueh prescribed more than sixty remedies, all of them graced with what Hsiung calls "enticing names." These included complex concoctions, food recipes, pills, cakes, powders, drinks, and so on. Many of the recipes for these medicines were converted into rhymed verses for easy memory and transmission so they could be broadly available.

The medical concern for men was not just limited to their sexual potency. The Chinese developed a whole branch of medicine concerned with men's health. It paralleled our gynecology, which focuses exclusively on women. Hsiung suggests we might call it andronology, and she points out that there is no parallel to this in other systems of medicine. One purpose of andronology was to improve the quality of offspring and to treat infertility. It also included contraceptive ways of lessening the chance of pregnancy. And these medical texts also urged "thriftiness in coital intercourse and seminal emission" to improve "the male essence" and make sex and reproduction more successful.

Conclusions on Sex and Family Planning

The Chinese approach to these subjects was religiously conditioned by the Taoist deep appreciation of nature, the Confucian reverence for moderation and loyalty to family, and the Buddhist advocacy of compassion and the inter-connectedness of all things. Good sex, "high sex," demands more than the release of an urge. It involves "morality, aes-thetics, and heavenly blessing." There was no contradiction in their view in saying that good sex involves pleasure and duty, celebration and moderation. In light of all this, Hsiung finds some of our Western ideas strange. She even calls them "ignorance fed by self-congratulatory arrogance."

What is she talking about? She is amazed that we tend to think we discovered sexual fun and pleasure in our so-called "sex revolution," and that this was only possible because of the invention of "the pill." The Chinese were into unabashed sexual fun from time immemorial. Also, she finds our Western debate between pro-life and pro-choice "mystifying and misleading." All human choices, she says, are made with life in view, and life is a series of choices. Confucianism and Taoism, she says, "have no inherent opposition to contraception or abortion." These are realities to be faced and are necessary at times to pre-serve the greater harmony of the world.

Reading Chinese scholars on sex and family planning reminds me of a moment in the past. I was at a conference with a number of Chinese and other scholars. One of these Chinese scholars was a witty woman who spotted me peek-ing into the lounge during a break to check on a football game. Knowing she could tweak me without breach of friendship, she said: "Ah, yes. That is a sport that would attract you adolescent Americans. When you mature you will delight in more delicate, less violent expressions of physical prowess, like ping-pong and gymnastics."

As we meet these older, experience-rich cultures, our Western attitudes toward sex and fertility are being tweaked and critiqued.

8. Judaism and Family Planning

JEWS, LIKE NATIVE AMERICANS, see population problems in a special way. Their up-close problem is depopulation, not overpopulation. As Jewish theologian Laurie Zoloth says: "Falling fertility rates among Jews and increasing intermarriage can be graphed to show a point a generation or two in the imagined future in which there will be no Jews at all." Jews have been through more than one holocaust and have repeated experiences of exile. That they have continued to exist at all as a discernible religious culture is amazing. Before the Nazi Holocaust, there were about 18 million Jews in the world; afterwards, the number was only 11 million. Elliott Dorff, an ethicist from the Conservative Jewish Movement, says:

> We as a people are in deep demographic trouble. We lost one-third of our numbers during the Holocaust. . . . The current Jewish reproductive rate among American Jews is between 1.6 and 1.7 [2.1 is considered replacement level]. That statistic means we are killing ourselves off as a people. . . . This social imperative has made propagation arguably the most important mitzvah [duty] of our time. . . . To refuse to try to have them, or to plan to have only one or two is to refuse to accept one of God's great gifts. It is also to renege on the duty we all have to create the next generation and to educate them in Torah.

In the United States, as of 1990, Jews who were once 3.7 percent of the population were only 2.4 percent. Of that number, 52 percent were intermarried to non-Jews, and only 25 percent of these were raising their children as

Jews. You can understand why family planning for Jews can mean planning to have more children, not fewer. And talk of abortion does not raise enthusiasm, even though most Jews are pro-choice. Immanuel Jakobowitz, the former Chief Rabbi of Britain, remarking on abortion in Israel, noted that "abortion deprived the Jewish state of over a million native-born citizens." Canadian Jewish scholar Sharon Joseph Levy says: "It has been estimated that a people this ancient, living continuously in its own homeland, without ever being exiled, would number one billion people."

If Judaism were only interested in the survival of Jewish people, we might well conclude that Judaism would not be of much help to us in addressing the overall world population problem. And yet Judaism never thought of numbers as its contribution to the world. Deuteronomy 7:7 makes this clear: "It was not because you were more numerous than any other people that the Lord set his heart on you and chose you—for you were the fewest of all peoples."

In fact, Judaism is an essential partner in the interreligious discussion of any moral issue. Judaism is the spiritual parent of Christianity and Islam and a major shaper of Western culture. As the historian of religions Morton Smith says, early Israel became "the seedbed of the subsequent religious history of the Western world." There can be no sophisticated study of Western culture that does not explore the massive influence of Judaism on us all. For Jews, the survival of Jews is not a motive standing by itself. It's what Jews have to offer that is important. Notice in the quote given above from Elliott Dorff that the last word is "Torah." The reason to have children was to teach them Torah and not to let the vision die. Torah can refer narrowly to the first five books of the Hebrew Bible, but it is used more generically to encapsulate the full richness of historical Jewish teaching.

Judaism did not begin as a religion in our modern sense of the word; their language didn't even have a word for religion. Judaism began as a workshop for a new humanity. They looked at the decaying societies around them and decided to rethink life from top to bottom. Early Israel constituted a "creative break from the past." The remarkable people who gathered together to form Israel three thousand years ago presented the world with a new philosophy of life. This is their not-at-all-modest self-portrait in Deuteronomy: "You will display your wisdom and understanding to other peoples. When they hear [this] they will say, 'What a wise and understanding people this great nations is!'" (4:6 NEB). These folks were not timid about their mission. They dared to think of themselves as "a light to the nations . . . to the end of the earth" (Isaiah 49:6). They believed they had a message, a Torah, that could save the world from its self-destructive ways.

All of this is beautifully recognized by the gifted writer Thomas Cahill, who is not a Jew himself. His book is titled *The Gift of the Jews* and is provocatively subtitled: *How a Tribe of Desert Nomads Changed the Way Everyone Thinks and Feels*. His opening lines are these: "The Jews started it all—and by 'it' I mean so many of the things we care about, the underlying values that make all of us, Jew and gentile, believer and atheist, tick. Without the Jews, we would see the world through different eyes, hear with different ears, even feel with different feelings." So what was this vision, this Torah, and how can it help us in dealing with the human need for contraception and for abortion as a backup when necessary?

In the Image of God

Laurie Zoloth, who is professor of Jewish studies at San Francisco State University, will be our principal guide in this chapter. Zoloth is a prolific scholar, an observant

Orthodox Jew, and—relevant to the Jewish demographic problem—the mother of five children. If we run out of Jews, it won't be Zoloth's fault. As our scholars worked on this family planning project, Zoloth took us through the fascinating history of how Jews have dealt with fertility questions. Before taking that short tour with her, let us look at some of the central teachings of Torah and see the relevance of each of them to our issues.

It's hard to sum up any major religion in a brief catechism, but let's try to hit some of the main points of Jewish moral and religious wisdom, looking at two things: (1) their casting humanity as "in the image of God"; (2) their rich and radical theory of justice. Each of these has an impact on the Jewish ethics of family planning.

Image of God is such a familiar term for many people that it might seem piously boring. In its origins, it started a revolution that continues into our day. *Image of God* was used by monarchs to shore up their authority in the world of the ancient Israelites. The king or pharaoh was the image of God, giving him divine rights. The Israelites stole the term and gave it a whole different meaning. They democratized it. They said: "If you want to see the image of God, look at the baby in my arms. That is the image of God. Look at my father sitting by the fire, hobbled by age. He is the image of God. Run to the reflecting pond and look at your face there. You are looking at the image of God." This undermined the idea of royalty. It set the stage for democratic theory in the West and things like the Bill of Rights in the U.S. Constitution.

Genesis connects this with reproduction: "So God created humans in his own image; in the image of God he created them: male and female he created them. God blessed them, and God said to them, 'Be fruitful and multiply, and fill the earth and subdue it'"(1:27-28). Interestingly, in Genesis, God also wanted the fish and the birds to multiply. With them, however, as Sharon Levy says, "the need to procreate is inbred. With people, procreation is a blessing and a directive: 'God said to them. . . . ' Human beings are not simply animals doing what comes naturally. We have a divine directive, and we can exercise self-control." The directives of God are not inscribed on our genes but directed to our power of reasoning and providing. Being the image of God makes us, again in Thomas Aquinas's terms, "participants in divine providence." We are to manage this fruitfulness and not reproduce without reason.

As Zoloth says, "we are not the ones who swarm over the earth" like insects. When you give birth to a human child, as Maimonides said, it is "as if a whole world is created." Childmaking is worldmaking—such is the value Judaism puts on every human life. In this supreme valuing of each individual, "it is particularity, and not abundance that is stressed."

Those who would use the Genesis "increase and multiply" text to justify the rejection of family planning do violence to a text that actually gives profound theological justification for family planning. The command to "increase and multiply" was given to beings gifted with reason, and so the increase and multiplication was to be reasonable. Also, in the Jewish view, quality counts more than quantity. We don't just make human beings, we are obligated to make *humane* human beings who can bring the message of Torah to the world. Which bring us to the Torah's teaching on justice.

The Hebrew word most used to convey the idea of justice, *Tzedaqah* (pronounced *say-dah-kah*), has more meaning than our word justice can contain. In its Aramaic root, it means mercy to the poor and the destitute. Hebrew justice means the usual duties of paying debts and fulfilling contracts, but its program is much broader. When Job defended his virtue, he spoke in *Tzedaqah* terms, claiming he had been "eyes to the blind, feet to the lame. I was a father to the needy"; he saved the orphan, the widow, and "the poor man when he called for help." He took up the cause of persons whom he did not even know (Job 29:12-20 NEB). In our terms, his justice was proactive, not just reactive. Saying that he had merely paid his bills would be no defense at all in this generous Hebraic notion of justice. This is the central message of Torah, and when you have children, you accept the vocation to make them doers and messengers of *Tzedaqah*. What is key, says Zoloth, is not fecundity or numbers of persons, but the enactment of justice. The common good is not created by women's ability to make many children but in her ability to create a household of justice. In such a household, her hands go out to her children, but she will also "stretch her hands out to the poor and her palms to the destitute."

Justice and justice-teaching are intrinsic to parenting in Judaism. Justice requires that families look out not only for themselves, but also that they make sure "ever larger families do not overwhelm a community's ability to care for the poor." Family planning is planning births so they can spread justice on the earth.

This Jewish linking of parenting and justice gives yet another theological basis for family planning. It also forbids a neo-Malthusian shrinking of the problems of the world down to numbers: "Too many people, that's all." Supporting birth control is not enough. Sharon Levy asks the tougher questions, questions filled with the spirit of *Tzedaqah*: "Would we support birth control efforts but not forge ahead with bringing justice to those in need? Would we be willing to modify our lifestyles for their sake and the sake of the world itself?" Condoms are not enough to fix this world. But, speaking of condoms, how do contraception and abortion when necessary as a back-up fit into Jewish ethics?

Contraception and Abortion

Realistic flexibility is the hallmark of any religion that appears and stays around for a long time. In Judaism, there is what Zoloth describes as "room for vigorous debate with contradictory opinions heard and honored." Since there was no "central authority," specific issues were always open for debate. Religions are concerned with life and how it is lived, and we humans are complex and always changing. For that reason, a religion is not just a collection of written scrolls. Each enduring religion represents, as Judaism does in Zoloth's term, "thousands of years of discourse." Judaism never saw religion as a remote backdrop. Again, Zoloth says: "It is the totality of life the Jewish belief is after—the inescapable call of the stranger, the constancy of the demand for justice in every interaction, and the importance of the minute details of daily life." Certainly, reproductive life was not going to be left out.

Like all the ancient religions, Judaism was pro-birth. It couldn't be stated more starkly than in the Tannaim in the Tosefa: "One who does not procreate both denies God and commits murder" (8:7). But right away, flexibility appears. After that blunt statement, the text goes on to excuse a man who is so taken up with the study of Torah that he has not taken the time to have children. Rather than condemn him as a murderer, he is seen as "an example of diligence and dedication to the study of Torah." In other words, the Genesis mandate to "be fruitful and multiply" involves more than making babies. There are other ways of being fruitful; there are other forms of "increase" and other goods to be multiplied. "Having students is akin to childbearing," Zoloth tells us. For humans, there are many forms of fertility. Justice, *Tzedaqah*, is the prime Jewish virtue, and being just may require limiting births. Limiting births may be necessary to do justice to the children we already have and to do justice to our community.

One old example of birth limitation concerns women who are nursing. The nursing mother had to use birth control to avoid pregnancy. The health of the nursing child who, the Rabbis thought, might be compromised by another pregnancy or even by full intercourse, was primary. Thus the *mokh*, a soft cotton pad worn internally against the cervix, was prescribed. Nursing was thought to be a two or even three-year period, and the ban against getting pregnant in this time was severe. The Talmud, a body of teaching dating back some fifteen hundred years, says that a divorcée or widow who is nursing or is pregnant (and will be nursing soon) cannot marry until her child is two years old. If she marries before that time, she must divorce and not remarry until the full twenty-four months pass.

The *mokh* was also permitted as a birth control method for other reasons, such as the well-being of the woman. Contraception is not forbidden in Judaism, even though fertility is seen as a precious divine gift.

And what of abortion? In the book of Exodus, there is a revealing case of accidental abortion. "When people who are fighting injure a pregnant woman so that there is a miscarriage, and yet no further harm follows, the one responsible shall be fined what the woman's husband demands, paying as much as the judges determine." (21:22 NRSV). This is the earliest clue that a fetus was not seen as having equal standing with a born person. The penalty here is a monetary fine. If the woman had died, it could be capital punishment, "a life for a life." The fetus was not yet a fully-fledged life—in our terms, not yet a person. Today, some call this "delayed ensoulment," as opposed to ensoulment, or personing, at conception. Fetal tissue is human but not yet personal.

This idea has continued in Judaism. In the ancient writings of Judaism, Zoloth tells us that "abortion is permitted as a health procedure since a fetus is not seen as being an ensouled person. Not only are the first forty days of conception considered 'like water' but also even in the last trimester, the fetus has a lesser moral status." The fetus is not deemed a *nefesh*, a person, until the head emerges in the birthing process (Rashi commenting on Sanhedrin 72b). Because of this teaching, there can be a variety of reasons justifying abortion. Avoiding disgrace is one justifying cause. An early modern response to abortion puts it this way: It states the ideal, which is not to destroy a fetus, but then it quickly adds, "Clearly it is not forbidden when it is done because of a [great] need." It addresses the predicament of a married woman who is pregnant from another man. "If there is no reason, it is forbidden to destroy the fetus. But in the case before us of a married woman who went astray, I have pronounced my lenient opinion that it is permitted to abort, and perhaps it even almost has the reward of a *mitzvah*" (Jacob Emden, *Responsa She'elat Ya'avetz,* No. 43).

Calling the abortion a *mitzvah* is significant. A *mitzvah* is a sacred duty. It is even customary to recite a blessing before doing a *mitzvah*: "Blessed are thou Lord God, King of the Universe who has sanctified us through your commandments. . . ." It is not a slight thing, then, to say that an abortion in these circumstances is a meritorious action, a sacred choice, not just something tolerated as a lesser evil.

Reasons of health are also grounds for abortion. The case was raised of a pregnant woman who had an ear infection; the doctors said that if she remained pregnant she could lose her hearing. The response was that deafness "will ruin the rest of her life, make her miserable all her days, and make her undesirable in the eyes of her husband. Therefore . . . she should be permitted to abort her fetus through highly qualified doctors who will guarantee ahead of time that her life will be preserved, as much as this is possible" (Ben Zion Uziel, Mishpetei Uziel, *Hoshen Mishpat* 3:46).

The rabbis also took on the case of craniotomy, very late-term abortion when the birthing process has already begun. The Talmud says: "If a woman suffers hard labor in travail, the child must be cut up in her womb and brought out piecemeal, for her life takes precedence over its life: if its greater part [head] has already come forth, it must not be touched, for the [claim of one] life cannot supersede [that of another] life" (*Mishneh* 6).

The views on all of these cases were broadly held by the community. We know this because of this principle of Jewish jurisprudence: "We do not make a ruling unless the majority of the community can abide by it" (*Baba Kama* 79b).

The Sanctity of Life

The Jewish religion, which has parental status for Christianity and Islam—all three are known as "the Abrahamic religions"—laid the cornerstone of respect for individual and social life in the Western world. Its idea that every single person is a child of God, made in the image of God, undergirds the ethical and legal conception of "the sanctity of life." It is highly significant, therefore, that it forthrightly addressed the issues of contraception and abortion when necessary. And it comes down firmly on allowing these moral freedoms.

Therefore, we see again that the right to choose an abortion has deep religious roots. Laws that deny women this right are unjust and violate religious freedoms. Such restrictive laws unduly privilege religious persons who espouse the most conservative views while disenfranchising those who hold equally religiously-grounded pro choice views. Governments that criminalize all abortions have taken sides in a religious debate. Since there are good religious authorities on both sides of the debate, government has no right to intrude.

9. The Wisdom of Islam

"CARICATURE ASSASSINATION" (a phrase coined by Protestant theologian Robert MacAfee Brown) is step one in ecumenical dialogue. It's not that we know nothing of other religions. We have impressions of them, but they are like photos taken from too far away. They are more caricatures than pictures, and sometimes when the truth arrives about these religions, we resist it. We've become too comfortable with the caricature. Often the caricature that we have about other religions is created by news stories on television and in the papers, stories focused on fringe groups and fanatics. Such stories and such people hide from us the gentle core of wisdom that is the true soul of all great religions.

I do not think that any religion suffers more from "bad press" and caricature than Islam. When my son, Tom, and his wife recently embraced the faith of Islam, some friends asked in revealing jest: "Are they building a bomb factory in their cellar?" The joke is on our common ignorance, not on the ancient faith of Islam. When the federal building was blown up in Oklahoma City in 1995, suspicion fell first on "Muslim fundamentalists," and persons with Arab features were looked for as the culprits. When the truth came out, there was Timothy McVeigh—sounding more like an Irish Catholic than an Arab Muslim.

Interestingly, the word Islam means peace and is related to the Hebrew *shalom*. The Qur'an (often written Koran), which Muslims believe to have been divinely revealed to Muhammad in the seventh century C.E., states the basis of

Islam in a single sentence: "We believe in God, and that which has been sent down on us, and sent down on Abraham and Ishmael, Isaac and Jacob, and the Tribes, and in that which was given to Moses and Jesus, and the Prophets of their Lord; we make no distinction between any of them, and to Him we surrender" (3:85). In other words, Muslims see themselves as relatives of Jews and Christians. Muhammad was trying to get back to the original purity of the religious and moral movement begun by Abraham. The moral goal of this faith is to see all peoples transformed into one family, one people—in the Arabic, one *umma,* filled with justice, peace and compassion. Muslims see themselves as God's *vicegerents* (deputies) on earth, put here to do the work that will bring peace and prosperity to all God's children.

Now having said that, mention the plight of women in the Muslim world. Or say the words Taliban, "Muslim fundamentalists," Salmon Rushdie, or "the Islamic Republic of Iran," and the words in the preceding paragraph seem unrelated and unreal. The most obvious truth in religious dialogue is this: Great faiths and the adherents of those great faiths do not always match. Christians are not Christian enough, Hindus are not Hindu enough, and Muslims are not Muslim enough. We are all unworthy heirs to the religious and moral traditions we inherited. We all love to profess great ideals, but living them is a burden we craftily eschew. Nations are the same as religions. In the United States, we boast of "equal justice for all," but who is naive enough to say that the same justice can be expected by the black and the white, by the well-heeled and the poor, by the well educated and the illiterate, by immigrants and citizens?

The Islamic scholars with whom I work are one and all devout Muslims. They are also all reformers, "liberation

theologians," feminists, and lovers of justice and peace.
One of them, Farid Esack, is the Minister for Gender
Equality in the government of South Africa. Another,
Asghar Ali Engineer, works in his Islamic Studies center in
the slums of Bombay, defending the rights of women and
the poor. Nawal Ammar, natively of Egypt, writes of the
true Islam that would end poverty and empower women.
The principal guide for this chapter, who worked on the
family planning project, is Riffat Hassan. Hassan, currently
a professor at the University of Louisville, is a native of
Pakistan. She is an activist as well as a scholar and works
in Pakistan and India. She has been particularly active in
fighting the "honor killings" of women that are tolerated in
much of the Muslim world.

Hassan is a feminist, and I love her definition of feminism. It is "a passionate quest for truth and justice on
behalf of women." Notice these words: Feminism is not
just an outlook or a set of ideas. It is not a view from the
sidelines. It is a passionate, activist pursuit of justice and
truth to end the victimization of women.

Hassan and these other scholars do not try to cover up
the current state of Islam. There are problems, and Hassan
is blunt in stating them. For example, regarding women in
Islamic countries, she says: "Women are regarded in virtually all Muslim societies as being less than fully human.
The way Islam has been practiced in most Muslim societies for centuries has left millions of Muslim women with
battered bodies, minds, and souls. These women have
been kept in physical, mental, and emotional bondage.
The rate of literacy of Muslim women, especially those
who live in rural areas where most of the population lives,
is among the lowest in the world." These words spoken by
a devout Muslim woman are not hedged or calculated to
excuse the weaknesses of Muslim societies. Muslim faith

requires an honest admission of sinfulness, and I assure my readers that the reformers in Islam—and they are many and everywhere in the Islamic world—are nothing if not honest. They rail against the injustices done in the name of Islam, and they are deeply pained at the distortion of their faith by some of their fellow Muslims that has gone too long unchallenged and unchanged.

Reformation: Back to the Core

Early Christians came up with the axiom *ecclesia semper reformanda*, "the church is always in need of reform." The ideals that gave birth to the great religions are like delicate flowers trying to take root but always getting crushed under foot. Rescuing those flowers is the reformer's mission. What are the flowers of Islam? What are the core moral values in Islamic ethics?

According to Muslim theologian Asghar Ali Engineer, the first answer to that question is obvious. Asghar Ali Engineer tells us, "the most fundamental values in Islam, as expounded by the Qur'an, are justice, benevolence, and compassion." The Qur'anic terminology for these values is *'adl, ihsan,* and *rahmah*. Any legislation, custom, or ruling by Islamic teachers that offends these values is invalid and un-Islamic. The insight here is that no family, no human institution, or no society will flourish unless it has these values as its cornerstone. But notice, justice does not stand alone; it is bonded to benevolence and compassion. Justice that is not ensouled by compassion becomes cold and rigid. Showing its continuity with Jewish and Christian morality, Islam insists that true justice, in Asghar Ali Engineer's words, shows "deep concern for the weaker sections of society. Verse 28:5 of the Qur'an expresses this concern and says: 'And We desire to bestow a favour upon those who were deemed weak in the land, and to make them leaders, and to make them the heirs.' The Qur'an desires to bestow the mantle of leadership of this earth upon those who are weak." One obvious conclusion of this, says Asghar Ali Engineer, is that "women certainly belong in this category in a patriarchal society." If one accepts the Qur'an, women are to be made "leaders and heirs."

This Islamic elevation of the weak to leadership roles should remind Christians of Jesus' words in Luke's Gospel: "Blessed are you poor for yours is the kingdom of God" (4:20 NEB). It should also recall Mary's *Magnificat*: "He has brought down the powerful from their thrones, and lifted up the lowly; he has filled the hungry with good things, and sent the rich away empty." (Luke 1:52-53 NRSV). At root, Jews, Christians, and Muslims are morally kin. Only the mess of history divides them.

This central stress on justice in Islam doesn't languish in generality. It gets down to the nuts and bolts of what justice means in real life. Hassan tells us:

> The Qur'an puts great emphasis on the preservation of what we today refer to as 'fundamental human rights' such as (a) the right to be respected for one's humanity [16]; (b) the right to be treated with justice and equity [17]; (c) the right to be free of abusive authority whether religious, intellectual, political or economic, and the right to be free of sexism and slavery, classism or caste-system [18]; (d) the right to privacy and protection from slander and ridicule [19]; (e) the right to learn and acquire knowledge [20]; (f) the right to private property and the right to work and earn a decent living [21]; (g) the right to move freely and to have a secure home [22,23]; (h) the right to one's aesthetic sensibilities, the right to enjoy and express the beauties of God's creation [24]; (i) the right not just to survive but to thrive and prosper [25].

And more. The Qur'an is the original "liberation theology." (It is easy to see why Islam has attracted so many African Americans. They find that, more than Christians, Muslims reject the color-caste poison of racism. And so Lou Alcindor became Abdul Jabbar, Cassius Clay became Mohammed Ali, and Malcolm X came back from Mecca with gentler views of race.)

You can understand the impatience of progressive Islamic scholars when they see how the grandeur of the Qur'anic vision has been squandered and corrupted in so many Muslim societies. And you can see why progressive Islamic scholars are not so much avant-garde as conservative and traditional. They're trying to get Islam back to its glorious origins just as the prophets of Israel did and, indeed, as all the reformers in all the religions are doing.

Zakat and Hay'a

Before turning to family planning and Islam's position on contraception with abortion as a backup when necessary, let us add to our Arabic vocabulary two words that give us a better view into the soul of Islam. *Zakat* literally means "sweetening." It also has connotations of "purifying." When applied to wealth, as Islamic scholar Isma'il R. Al-Faruqi says, "it means making that wealth 'sweet', i.e. just, legitimate, innocent, good and worthy. Obviously what *zakat* adds to wealth is not utilitarian, but moral." Islam has no objection to the accumulation of wealth, but it insists that all wealth must be shared to be moral, to be "purified." The purpose of sharing is the utter elimination of poverty in the *ummah*, in the community. Hassan tells us that "according to the Qur'an, one should give away (as *zakat*) 'whatever is beyond' our needs. However, Sunni Muslims mostly accept the percentage of two-and-a-half percent, determined by classical jurists as the amount of annual *zakat*." This was the way the Prophet Muhammad created a welfare society in which the needs of all were met. It made "wealth sharing" a pillar of faith.

Thus good Muslims will be generous in charitable giving, but beyond their private charity, *zakat* requires that they give 2.5 percent of *their total wealth*—not their annual income!—for distribution to the poor. Add up the value of your home, your investments, and all superfluous belongings (including your jewelry), and give 2.5 percent of that a year as *zakat*. Like the Hebrew-Jewish tradition, Islam regards all wealth and even our lives as belonging to God, and God forbids the coexistence of poverty and wealth. Every person created by God is so good and so precious that they deserve not just adequacy, but a comfortable and even a prosperous life.

This sets the tone for the Islamic view of family planning. Individual rights are set in a context of social conscience and social obligation. The stress on a generous adequacy for all means that quality of offspring is more important than quantity. If the population exceeds natural resources, there can be no comfortable or prosperous life.

Islamic teaching mandates respect for all people. "Never will I suffer to be lost the work of any of you be he male or female. Ye are members of one another, and behave with *hay'a* toward them" (Ali Imran: 195). *Hay'a*, Ammar tells us, is a word so rich that it cannot be translated by a single word. In her view, it reflects an attitude of gentle reverence and respect for all of God's creation. It seems to connote a sense of wonder and gratitude in the face of the unearned gift of existence. Ammar translates it as "dignified reserve" and shows how it dictates an ecological ethic and a sense of limit. It is a word that can be extended and applied to family planning. We should respect the right of all children to have a comfortable and

a prosperous life, to develop all of their talents and aes-
thetic potential. *Hay'a* demands that we do not produce
more children than we can provide for generously.

Note well, however, that Islam is not saying that poverty
comes only from overpopulation. *Zakat* shows that the
main evil is the lack of distribution of wealth rather than the
presence of too many people. Overconsumption and gluttony are targeted more than overreproduction. It is the
unsharing rich more than the overreproducing poor that
Islam hits with prophetic critique, though it recognizes the
human right to and need for family planning. Overreproduction is bad; not sharing is worse.

Contraception and Abortion in Islam

Islam's views on family planning are important for our
planet, since one out of every six people on this earth is a
Muslim. We can say from the outset that there is pluralism in the Muslim world (as there is everywhere). There
are conservatives, liberals, and those who claim to be
centrists. No major religion is a grid into which all the
faithful neatly fit. In approaching Islam, it is necessary
to see what the teaching authority structure is. Clearly,
the Qur'an is the prime authority, considered divine revelation. But the authority of the Qur'an is not magical.
Al-Faruqi makes the interesting point that Muslims do
not claim any miracles for Muhammad to shore up the
authority of the Qur'an. "The Qur'anic revelation is a pre-
sentation to one's mind, to reason." There is no papal figure or ruling synod in Islam that can impose its views. "In
Islam, religious truth is a matter of argument and conviction, a cause in which everybody is entitled to contend and
everybody is entitled to convince and be convinced." Certain institutions, like the Al-Azhar University in Cairo,
have a lot of teaching prestige, and the opinions and pro-

nouncements of certain authoritative persons have a lot of weight, but their weight is not so heavy as to crush personal conscience.

Also, as Hassan points out, the Qur'an is not "an encyclopedia which may be consulted to obtain specific information about how God views each problem, issue or situation." It is not a blueprint for moral life covering all the questions from the seventh to the twenty-first century and beyond. For this reason, there are other sources of truth in Islam. The *Hadith* are sayings attributed to the Prophet Muhammad. These do not all agree, and the authenticity of many is doubted and debated. The *Sunnah* are the practical traditions rising out of the life of Muhammad. There is also the huge body of legal literature known as *Shari'ah*, which again is contradictory at times. Some of its regressive and antiwoman prescriptions are preferred by right-wing zealots. However, the Qur'an is the Supreme Court, and its central values, outlined above, hold sway over any later interpretation. The prime value there, as we saw, is justice animated with mercy and respect for all persons. Whatever contradicts that is not true to Islam.

There is another principle in Islamic teaching that is central to Muslim ethics. It is called *ijithad*. This is the heart of any true religious ethic. It means that you analyze the unique data of a current moral problem, and argue from Qur'anic principles, using analogy and logic to come to the best and most reasonable solution. As the jurist and philosopher Azizah Y. al-Hibri says, this gave Islamic ethics great flexibility. "It is an essential part of Qur'anic philosophy, because Islam was revealed for all people and for all times." It allows Islamic ethics to respond realistically to new problems for which there is no spelled-out answer in the Qur'an. It established Islam's respect for our faculty of reason.

In Islam, as in all the religions, fertility is highly prized, and children are a gift of God to bring "joy to our eyes" (Surah 25: Al-Furqan: 74). Conservatives argue that family planning is a lack of trust in the sustaining God. They cite texts such as this: "There is no creeping being on earth but that upon God is its sustenance" (Surah 11: Hud: 6). The Qur'an also says that if we place our trust in God, that is enough. I quoted my mother's Irish faith earlier, saying that God will not send a child without sending the means to feed it.

This naive and passive trust that no matter what we do or don't do, God will make up the difference, does not bear scrutiny and does not face up to the perennial fact of starving children. It is dismissed by Islam's best theologians. Theologian Fazlur Rahman says that using the Qur'anic references to God's power and promise to sustain all creation to argue "for an unlimited population out of proportion to the economic resources is infantile. The Qur'an certainly does not mean to say that God provides every living creature with sustenance whether that creature is capable of procuring sustenance for itself or not." We are not passive sheep waiting to be fed, in the Islamic view. We are God's vicegerents on earth, gifted with reason and talent. God has shared responsibility for providence with us and has given us the power to be prudent, to see problems and do something sensible about them.

(It is always interesting to see similarities among the different religions. These Islamic views on providence square beautifully with Thomas Aquinas's description of humans as "participants in divine providence." Also, in Catholic theology, relying on God's sustaining power to do what we have been equipped by God to do for ourselves is called the sin of "tempting God.")

Contraception has a long history in Islam. Early Islam actually developed contraceptive medicine and instructed

Europe on it. Avicenna, the Muslim physician, discusses in his book *The Law* twenty different substances used for birth control. Such Islamic books of medicine were used for centuries in Europe. When Europe was in its Dark Ages, Islamic culture, with its stress on education, kept the light of learning burning to the benefit of all peoples.

The most common form of birth control when Islam began was called *azl*, withdrawal (coitus interruptus). There are five major schools of law in Islam, and all five permit the practice of *azl*; four of the five insist that the consent of the wife is necessary. And here is where *ijtihad* comes in, reasoning analogically from something already permitted. The Arab Republic of Egypt published a booklet called "Islam's Attitude toward Family Planning." They state in its introduction that broad consultation with the most authoritative sources in Islam went into the research on this book. After noting that *azl* is permitted, they argue that any method that has the same purpose as *azl* and does not induce permanent sterility is acceptable for Muslims. They then go on to list methods such as the cervical cap, the condom, contraceptive pills, injections to produce temporary sterility, and the "loop device" placed in the uterus to prevent implantation of the fertilized egg.

There are many reasons in Islam that justify contraception: reasons of health, economics, the preservation of the woman's appearance, and improving the quality of offspring. This last reason is important in Islam, because the Islamic approach to contraception has a social conscience. It is concerned with the common good. Producing sickly, weak, or underdeveloped or uneducated children is not good for the *umma*, the society. The Egyptian study says that "the strength of a nation is measured not by numbers or quantities, but rather by quality." The study stresses the importance "of being rational and moderate and of living within the possible means and available resources." The *hadith* literature also says it is better to have few who are virtuous than many who are not. Once again, human life deserves to thrive, not just to eke out a living.

What then about sterilization? In blessing the use of contraceptives, we saw the precondition that none of them cause permanent sterility. There is a wisdom in this. It is senseless to permanently sterilize if temporary sterility would meet the needs of the situation. Having stated the Islamic opposition to permanent sterilization, the Egyptian study immediately moves to exceptions and says that if the husband or wife suffer from a contagious or hereditary disease, permanent sterility is needed and moral. The study then invokes the principle of the lesser evil. This means that you may have objections to sterilization, but at times it will do less harm and is to be preferred. Interestingly, Catholic theologians today are using that same "lesser evil" argument to justify the use of condoms to prevent the spread of AIDS. Even the Vatican is showing some flexibility on this.

And then we come to abortion. There are those in Islam who oppose all abortions. A favored text to support this is: "Do not kill your children for fear of poverty for it is We who shall provide sustenance for you as well as for them" (Surah 6: At-Talaqa: 2–3). Hassan notes on this text that the reference is to killing already born children— usually girls. The text was condemning this custom. Also, she notes the Arabic word for killing in this text "means not only slaying with a weapon, blow or poison, but also humiliating or degrading or depriving children of proper upbringing and education." So once again, as in other religions, a text is being freighted with meaning that it cannot sustain. The text doesn't explicitly address abortion and therefore doesn't close the argument on it.

So the *no choice* view is not the prevailing view in Islam. There is broad acceptance in the major Islamic schools of law on the permissibility of abortion in the first four months of pregnancy. Most of the schools that permit abortion insist that there must be a serious reason for it, such as a threat to the mother's life or the probability of giving birth to a deformed or defective child. However, as the Egyptian study says: "Jurists of the Shiite Zaidiva believe in the total permissibility of abortion before life is breathed into the fetus, no matter whether there is a justifiable excuse or not." That would be a pure form of what some call "abortion on demand."

What about abortion after four months? Once again, it is a case of a rule against it but then the allowance of exceptions. The Egyptian study puts it this way: Abortion after four months is permissible "if there is an inevitable necessity such as fear of a difficult delivery and a trustworthy physician finds that the continuation of pregnancy would harm the mother." They justify such late abortion again by the use of the principle of "the lesser evil" or lesser harm. They even justify what is basically infanticide "when delivery becomes difficult and the preservation of the mother's life requires the cutting off of the fetus before it is taken out from the mother's uterus." Where medical care is good, such crises may usually be avoidable. But medicine is not good in all of the Islamic world, and Islamic ethics is realistic.

Because conservative voices have been louder in much of the world, religion is seen as the enemy of family planning. Properly understood, it is not. The Islamic Egyptian study reaches the opposite conclusion: "The best way to regulate the family is to understand religion well and to make this understanding prevail among all members of the nation." That is precisely the argument of this book. The importance of religion in national family planning efforts is illustrated by the successes in Indonesia, Bangladesh, and Iran. In all three nations, the religious leaders supported the family planning effort. In other Islamic countries, family planning programs have fared badly despite large international investments. So, once again, the argument of this book is that religion is an essential motivational force for successful family planning. If the false impression that all religions are opposed to family planning is allowed to go unchallenged, efforts in this area will fail. It's that simple.

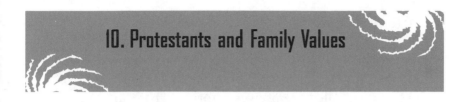

10. Protestants and Family Values

NO ONE WOULD DENY that the United States is a huge force on planet Earth. For better or for worse, we export a lot of culture (and subculture). Therefore, it is wise to know the forces that shape that complex thing called the "American mind." Open that mind, and you will see a lot of the phenomenon called Protestantism. Most Americans identify themselves as Protestant—56 percent. Catholics come in at 28 percent and Jews at only 2 percent. Beyond that, there are growing sprinklings of Buddhists, Muslims, Hindus, and others. Only 10 percent claim no religious affiliation at all. So as Italy, Spain, Ireland, and the Latin American countries can be legitimately called Catholic nations, the United States is Protestant.

So where are these Protestants when it comes to family planning? Their numbers alone suggest that they are going to be a major influence on reproductive ethics, public policy, and law.

Our guide here is Beverly Harrison, until recently professor of Christian Ethics at Union Theological Seminary in New York, now ensconced in the hills of North Carolina. Harrison tells us that "Protestant Christianity" includes a veritable "polyphony of Christian movements." Just as there are multiple Catholicisms and Hinduisms, there are many diverse Protestantisms. The term *Protestant* is used most generically to signify those Christian churches that do not accept the Roman Catholic authority system and are not affiliated with the Eastern Orthodox traditions.

To really get a fix on Protestantism, Harrison says, go back to the sixteenth century when the Protestant Reformation was launched. That century was marked by a number of movements against papal authority, movements that called themselves reforms. These movements gradually coalesced into discernible groupings. The earliest were led by Luther and took definite form in the German-speaking regions of Central Europe and Scandinavia. Ulrich Zwingli and John Calvin led the Swiss reforms. These predominantly Swiss churches came to be known as the "Reformed churches." A more radical European stream stressing personal faith rose out of farming and peasant communities, and its followers became known as Anabaptists. As the European empires moved over the world, they carried some of all these movements with them. Episcopalians in the United States generated a division led by John Wesley that became known as Methodism. Anabaptist movements emphasizing the priesthood of all believers and the local autonomy of congregations sprouted into the various Baptist congregations. And the diversification continues.

Amid all this diversity, Harrison says, the main uniting theme of Protestantism was based on "shifting the locus of theological teaching authority from hierarchical control of doctrinal interpretation to something like shared discernment in reinterpreting doctrine and morals." The protest of Protestantism was against mind control in faith and morals. There was no one *magisterium* before which all should bow. Protestantism tumbled to the fact that there are a lot of good people who see things differently. In Harrison's words, there are "complex alternative ways of being religious and Christian." Flexibility, and a certain openness to pluralism in religion and in ethics, was the fruit of this.

The Fundamentalist Temptation

The desire for simple, absolute truth is a constantly-beckoning security blanket, and not all Protestants could resist the allure. We see this today in those called right-wing fundamentalists. The term fundamentalist is tossed about promiscuously, but Harrison sees the nub of it in an "insistence on a religious monopoly of knowledge grounded in fear of alternative knowledges, particularly 'scientific' modes of knowledge generated in modernity, which the 'God-knowledge' people cannot control." Fear, then, is at the very pulse of fundamentalism. There is a lot of Protestant fundamentalism in the United States and increasingly in Latin America—to the point where it has the pope and others very worried about the loss of these Latin American "Catholic countries."

Cherchez la femme ("look for the woman") finds an application here. Part of fundamentalism is a reaction to the emergence of free women and the loss of male monopoly. In Harrison's view, "fundamentalism always involves the reinscribing of male supremacy within religion."

How does all this shake out on our family planning issues?

Contraception and Abortion

Protestantism was not born out of thin air but out of history. As a protest, it rejected much of that history but not all. It absorbed from that history the sporadic condemnations of abortion which rose on the crest of a strong historical antisexual asceticism that afflicted Christianity. This antisexual asceticism was somewhat understandable in light of the perceived moral laxity of the Roman Empire. It was a Christian reaction to the excesses of Roman culture, but these rigid and fear-ridden views on sex became part of Christian orthodoxy. This negativity to sex affected attitudes on abortion. Harrison says, "careful readings of the early Christian history of debate about abortion make clear that one primary reason for the occasional condemnations of abortion in theological sources, including early versions of Canon Law, was that women who had abortions were assumed invariably to be adulteresses."

As we saw in chapter 3 on Catholicism, there was not much theorizing about the ethics of abortion. It was more in the nature of an inherited taboo, handed down like an heirloom. It can be seen as an un-thought-out reflex that saw abortion as part of the sordid sexual agenda. The Reformation inherited this taboo legacy. Those early Protestant leaders who discussed abortion were against it—Calvin, for example, scathingly so. But, Harrison says, "explicit moral reasoning on why it was evil was lacking."

Exit Celibacy

Early Protestantism was a huge shift from the controlled church to a family-centered Christianity. Luther shut down monasteries and nunneries when he could, married a former nun, and ended the practice of clerical celibacy, a practice that was often more observed in the breach anyway. Zwingli and others joined in. Calvin declared that marriage is the preferred form of Christian faithfulness. One obvious result: Clergy living in a family setting, unlike monks in a monastery, had firsthand experience of the dilemmas of reproduction. They were in a position to learn that fertility could be either a blessing or a curse. (A pope who listened to his wife and children might be the wiser for it.) By a natural kind of development, then, Protestantism from the start was not resistant to family planning, even while it still held onto conservative religious views. Protestant birth rates showed that they were managing their fertility. Aside from its fundamentalist streams, Protestantism has been a sane and positive influence in family planning.

Move to the eighteenth and nineteenth centuries, and once again, Harrison says, you find both silence and sympathy on the birth control front. Reproductive health was being handled in "the women's health care culture," and women generally and midwives particularly saw the need for family planning. Men had not yet seized control of medicine.

In the nineteenth century, two things happened. An unhealthy, sexist kind of *sexual identity* that defined women in a limiting way began to be socially constructed, and it took hold, especially in fundamentalist segments of Protestantism. Secondly, male doctors were on the scene now, discouraging the midwives (who were their competition) and condemning abortion, something done by these midwives. Interestingly, the doctors did not have much success with Protestant leaders, who were reluctant to march in the anti-choice crusade.

By the end of the nineteenth century, feminism was rising and spreading to Protestant women and a few good men. The ordination of women changed the face of the clerical world and its male-centered mind-set. In all of this, we can see that religions don't just shape cultures; they are shaped by cultures. They respond like barometers to the climate around them. This is why religions are in constant need of reformation. A lot of what they absorb is toxic. Harrison tells us: "Some Protestant theologians embraced dubious 'scientific' teaching on eugenics because it held out [the] promise of 'race-lifting,' leaving out concern for the common good or the well-being of women. . . . Racist motives have sometimes shaped Protestant enthusiasm for population management and for birth control and abortion." This has not, however, been the main thrust of Protestantism.

The Christian Right and the Abortion Wars

The Christian right's new interest in abortion has been stimulated by an obvious agenda to resist any gender role shifts and advocacy for women's rights. Harrison points out that the new right-wing Christian demonology contains many devils: "feminists and women who have abortions or seek to keep abortion legal and also 'queers'—gays, lesbians, and other 'sexual nonconformists.'" The Protestant Christian right borrows freely from Roman Catholic conservatives in what Harrison calls "the new social construction of the fetus as 'person.'" They have been enormously successful. Again, Harrison: "Truly one of the most remarkable efforts in information control in human history has moved U.S. public discourse into an atmosphere in which any moral analysis of fetal life is suspect. Our public debate images the well-being of early gestating fetuses powerfully as 'the innocent unborn.' The well-being of a pregnant woman, willingly or unwillingly pregnant, is hardly mentioned."

The odd couple of current abortion politics is the Catholic hierarchy and right-wing Protestants. Together they have created an atmosphere that spawns fanaticism and even terrorism. In 1973, the Catholic bishops, for the first time in modern U.S. history, called for civil disobedience to resist laws legalizing abortion. In 1975, they pushed for a *single-issue* politics, urging Catholics to oppose any political candidate who supported the legalization of abortion. This was music to right-wing Protestant ears; they were also reeling from the *Roe v. Wade* decision on abortion. The healthier Catholic and Protestant traditions of social justice and concern for the poor and for peace were swallowed up in what I call *pelvic politics*.

There is ample reason to say that this newborn love of fetuses is but a cover for the patriarchal fear of the free woman who is appearing in our day. Can we really believe that patriarchal Catholics, patriarchal Protestants, and patriarchal Muslims, after centuries of warring with one another, are suddenly and stunningly bonded by fetus-love? (As we've seen, not all adherents of these religions can be branded as patriarchal.) Are not such improbable alliances always suspect? (One thinks of the text in Luke: "That same day Herod and Pilate became friends with each other; before this they had been enemies" [23:12 NRSV].) A question is a terrible thing to waste, and any analysis of the current anti-choice religious movements that ducks these questions about anti-choice fervor and fear of free women is purblind.

What lurks beneath family value rhetoric on the right—among Protestants and Catholics—is a kind of sweet love ethic that loses sight of social justice and the needs of the common good. This makes the right the darling of the harsher modes of capitalism. The suppression of social conscience and concern for the poor that is masked by family value piety, really intends, in Harrison's view, "to make Christianity the 'handmaiden' of 'the Market God' who brooks no rivals." Once again, she is on target.

The Bottom Line

Protestantism, the dominant religious affiliation in the United States and in many countries, is firmly in favor of family planning. However noisy the conservative minority may be, statements from the denominations are clear. Unfortunately, they haven't been loud, and a lot of people and politicians have never heard them. Let's hear a representative few.

The Religious Coalition for Reproductive Choice in Washington, D.C. (http://www.rcrc.org) has done us the favor of gathering official position statements from U.S. religious bodies. What these statements prove is that the right to choose an abortion is a religiously-grounded right. If laws remove this right, they are taking sides in a religious debate where they have no right to meddle. And they are denying one side of the debate their civil liberties and religiously-grounded human rights.

The General Board of the American Baptist Churches pointed out in 1988 that there are legitimate differences among their members. Some oppose all abortion. "Many others advocate for and support family planning legislation, including legalized abortion as being in the best interest of women in particular and society in general." Both are good Baptists. No law should side with one religious position against the other, though both sides are free to advocate and debate in the public forum. Laws that take sides in the religious debate are guilty of partiality. They violate the human right to religious freedom.

In 1970 and again in 1989, the American Friends Service Committee stated their support for "a woman's right to follow her own conscience concerning child-bearing, abortion and sterilization. . . . That choice must be made free of coercion, including the coercion of poverty, racial discrimination, and the availability of service to those who cannot pay." No one can doubt the Quaker commitment to the sanctity of life, but they see the sanctity of life as requiring the right to choose an abortion when life's complexities make that the most pro-life choice.

In 1975 and again in 1989, the Disciples of Christ General Assembly resolved to "respect differences in religious beliefs concerning abortion and oppose, in accord with the principle of religious liberty, any attempt to legislate a specific religious opinion or belief concerning abortion upon all Americans."

how it should be

Legislators and judges, take heed. There is a strong consensus that the right to choose an abortion is religiously orthodox. Those religious people who think all abortions are wrong should not have abortions. Those religious people who believe on the basis of their religious tradition that they do have the right to choose should not have their religious freedom curtailed. It is a fascistic impulse to impose one moral view when there is no consensus and when good authorities disagree for good reasons.

!

this is what we do!

In 1988, the Episcopal Church General Convention defended "the legal right of every woman to have a medically-safe abortion." The Episcopal Women's Caucus insisted in 1978 that "the particular belief of one religious body should not be forced on those who believe otherwise." They also called for public funding of abortions for the poor. The Convocation Gathering of the Lutheran Women's Caucus in 1990 praised the "Religious Coalition for Reproductive Choice, a coalition of religious groups whose members hold diverse views about abortion and value the religious freedom that allows this diversity." The Northern Province of the Moravian Church in American in 1974 noted that "the Bible does not speak directly to the matter of abortion and the Moravian Church has refrained from being dogmatic when a biblical position was not clear."

good

The Presbyterian Church (USA), in five of its General Assembly meetings, approved of abortion until the fetus is viable. The Assembly approved "a public policy of elective abortion, regulated by the health code, not the criminal code. . . . Abortion should be a woman's right because, theologically speaking, making a decision about abortion

wow – PCUSA

is, above all, her responsibility." The statement "affirms the 1973 *Roe v. Wade* decision of the Supreme Court which decriminalized abortion during the first two trimesters of pregnancy."

The Reorganized Church of Jesus Christ of Latter Day Saints (RLDS) in 1974 and again in 1980 affirmed "the right of the woman to make her own decision regarding the continuation or termination of problem pregnancies." The Unitarian Universalist Association, in their General Assembly, stated in their 1963 meeting and in seven subsequent meetings "the personal right to choose in regard to contraception and abortion." They grounded this right in the prerogatives of "individual conscience" and they linked it to the "inalienable rights due to every person."

The United Church of Christ, in its General Synod 16, 1987, urged that "alternatives to abortion always be fully and carefully considered," but they then insisted that "abortion is a social justice issue . . . [requiring access to] safe, legal abortions." The United Methodist Church General Conference rejected in 1988 "the simplistic answers to the problem of abortion which, on the one hand, regard all abortions as murders, or, on the other hand, regard all abortions as procedures without moral significance. . . . We believe that a continuance of a pregnancy which endangers the life or health of the mother, or poses other serious problems concerning the life, health, or mental capability of the child to be, is not a moral necessity." In such cases, "mature Christian judgment may indicate the advisability of abortion." They explicitly support, as do many of these churches, the 1973 *Roe v. Wade* decision on abortion.

Respectable Debate

In a pluralistic, democratic society, issues supported by mainstream humanitarian and religious authorities, based on reasons that appeal to many people of good will and *sound judgment, <u>should not be banned by law.</u>* This can be called the principle of respectable debate.

The respectable debate criteria are not met if zoologi-cally-untrained people want to keep serpents in their churches to test their faith, as some sectarians do, and so this practice can be forbidden. The respectable debate cri-teria are not met if people decide for religious reasons to keep their children illiterate or deprive them of essential medicine. The right to contraception and to abortion when needed enjoys massive mainstream religious and humanitarian support, based on good reasons that appeal to many good and sensible people. In a truly democratic society, this right is inalienable.

The Common Good

Law requires an underlying consensus. The American experience with Prohibition illustrates this clearly. Augus-tine and Thomas Aquinas both thought prostitution was immoral, but both of them thought it should be legal. They judged that, given the realities of their society, there would be *mala inundantia*, a flood of evil results, if this practice were outlawed. <u>Lawmakers, like God, must toler-ate things for the common good that they themselves think evil.</u> Taking advice from these saints (who are part of the Christian and not just the Catholic legacy), lawmakers today who disapprove of all abortions can still, in good conscience, support the legalization and decriminaliza-tion of abortion. There is solid mainstream religious and humanitarian support for the right to choose an abortion. An attempt to outlaw this religious freedom of choice would not be successful. It would be Prohibition II. From the Protestant perspective, it would be an un-Protestant thing to do. It would reestablish the tyranny of con-science against which Protestant reformers, to their glory, protested.

11. Lessons from Native Religions

COLUMBUS DID NOT DISCOVER AMERICA. When the Europeans arrived—Native Americans call it "the European invasion"—there were more than a million people who had already lived in America for fifteen to twenty thousand years. And they didn't think the land needed to be rediscovered.

These people varied enormously. It is estimated that there may have been some two thousand different Native American cultures in North America when the Europeans arrived. According to many scholars, these people of Mongoloid stock seem to have entered the new world by crossing the Bering Strait during the last glacial period. For the most part, they had been living in harmony with their environment, doing some agriculture, fishing, and hunting. Harmony, social and environmental, was not what the Europeans brought with them. Genocide and the crushing of native cultures awaited the native residents of North America.

Historian David E. Stannard argues that "the destruction of the Indians of the Americas was, far and away, the most massive act of genocide in the history of the world." A nation that likes to think of itself as "kind and gentle" has this to live with. Native American population expert Russell Thornton estimates that at the nadir of American Indian population decline in the United States, only about 7 percent of the aboriginal population remained.

North American natives might therefore seem to be the least likely people to approach for religious wisdom on family planning. As with the Jews, depopulation has been their problem. As the Lakota holy man Lame Deer put it:

> The population explosion doesn't worry us much.
> All these long years, when the only good Indian was
> a dead Indian, the bodies at Wounded Knee, the Sand
> Creek Massacre, the Washita, all this killing of
> women and children, the measles and small pox wip-
> ing out whole tribes—the way I see it, the Indians
> have already done all the population control one
> could ask of them a hundred times over. Our prob-
> lem is survival. Overpopulation—that's your worry.

There are other reasons why Native Americans might seem unlikely resources for our topic in this book. Native women suffered from what Native writer and activist Andrea Smith calls "sexual colonization." European and American men regularly targeted them for sexual violence and death, using sexual assault as a way of subordinating the indigenous women and their communities. Men who interfered with the raping Spanish soldiers were killed. One of the consequences of this sexual reign of terror was syphilis, and it was devastating.

This abuse of Native women did not stop after the early invasion. It was discovered in the 1970s that the branch of the U.S. government responsible for Native health ser-vices, the Indian Health Service, was performing steriliza-tions on Native women without their consent. Connie Uri, the Choctaw/Cherokee doctor who discovered this, esti-mates that more than a quarter of all Native women had been forcibly sterilized in this way. Charon Astoyer, of the Native American Women's Health Education Resource Center, says that the use today of the contraceptives Depo-Provera and Norplant in American Indian communities can be seen as part of the unending assault. How, we might wonder, can such a brutalized people help us in mat-ters of reproductive health and planning?

Our special guide who will help us address this question is Mary Churchill, part of whose lineage is Cherokee.

Churchill is a professor of Native American Studies at the University of Colorado at Boulder. Churchill acknowledges all of the above, including Lame Deer's main point about overpopulation not being the Native's problem. However, she takes exception to his sweeping away of the problem. She says: "Global overpopulation is necessarily a Native concern." Lame Deer spoke of "all this killing of women and children," but as Churchill says, that killing "continues today, only in more subtle ways." The battering the earth is taking, sometimes magnified by the sheer mass of people, is global in its impact. There is no hideaway. If you flee for respite to the sweetest and loneliest little spot in the north woods, where the only sound is that of chirping birds and cackling crickets, the poisons still get to you and to the trees and the animals.

yes.

I was in the Black Forest in Germany some years ago, and I had a feeling of distance from the world and its problems. Then I ran into a sign hung by a hiker: *Der Wald stirbt,* the forest is dying. And it was. I could see it: trees poisoned by the rains that nourished them and the winds that whistled through the leaves.

Stories to Live By

Why do we go to a decimated people to talk about family planning? Because the lack of family planning is not an isolated problem. It is linked to a whole set of human behaviors and traits—greed, overconsumption, colonialism, racism, and militarism. The human problem is a sickness of the spirit; overpopulation is only one part of a broader malady. And it is here that Native Americans have a lot to say. As the Six Nations Iroquois Confederacy puts it: "Spiritual consciousness is the highest form of politics." They are saying: as your spirituality, so your behavior. Spirituality refers to what we hold sacred. In that sense, even materialism is a twisted kind of spirituality. What it

!

not in America

holds sacred is selfish accumulation. The Iroquois Confederacy is using the term in its positive sense, referring to civilizing values like gratitude, reverence for life, compassion, justice, and so forth. Our spirituality is measured by how much we love these values, and our love for these values (or lack of it) determines our politics.

Every culture has a set of values and its own sense of what is sacred, that is, what matters most. Buddhist philosopher David Loy makes the point that a new spirituality or religion is now spreading across the planet, seeping into culture after culture. This new religion is doing what the old religions always did: setting value priorities, saying what and who counts, providing a worldview. This new religion is setting the story line for our global community. The name of this religion, Loy says, is market capitalism. Capitalistic entrepreneurship is not intrinsically evil, but the current global capitalism carries a creed with it that is devastating to both the earth and humankind. Economics is the theology of this new religion, says Loy, "and its god, the Market, has become a vicious circle of ever-increasing production and consumption by pretending to offer a secular salvation. . . . The Market is becoming the first truly world religion, binding all corners of the globe into a worldview and set of values whose religious role we overlook only because we insist on seeing it as 'secular.'"

Yikes!

Religion never goes away. If one form of religion weakens, another takes it place. We need a true, humanizing religion or spirituality—the two words are almost synonymous. Humanity needs a new politics, a new way of doing business in the world. And here is where the rich cultures of Native America come to the fore. Says Churchill: "The experiences and perspectives of American Indians have the potential to reframe the population question entirely. Only after creating a new frame of reference, a new paradigm, can we consider in an ethical way the Native American religious resources that could justify the right to family planning, contraception, and abortion."

Malthus and Storytelling

Native Americans put enormous stress on the story, and the storyteller is something like a civil servant in their cultures. Says Churchill: "In much the same way as Westerners believe that money sets events into motion, American Indians believe that stories do not merely mirror reality; they create it." Churchill applies this to population. Malthus, she says, was "a storyteller *par excellence.*" Over two hundred years ago, he told a story of overpopulation, and the world has never been the same since. This is but one proof of the power of a story to grip human imagination and control us. The Malthusian error that Churchill cites is the belief that "overpopulation is the major cause of hunger, poverty, environmental destruction, and resource depletion and many other social, political, and economic ills. There is a growing number of scholars who contend that we are in the grip of that story." Environmentalist Betsy Hartmann supports the power of Malthus the storyteller. "So pervasive are Malthusian assumptions that many of us have internalized them without even realizing it." The heart of that seductive story is to blame the numbers, especially the number of poor people, while overlooking all the other iniquities messing up the world.

Asoka Bandarage agrees, saying that

> it can be argued that Malthusianism has shaped modern consciousness, determining the moral spirit of our age. . . . Population management by itself does not lead to the alleviation of poverty, environmental destruction, political unrest or other social problems. On the contrary, population management without

poverty alleviation, environmental restoration, and demilitarization results in the exacerbation of the existing problems and the victimization of poor women.

Powerful stories are the vehicle of a spiritual outlook and worldview. The Natives are right; we are in the grip of stories we have never examined, stories that control our politics, stories that are suffocating us.

Ingredients for a New Story

The prime story of the Native Americans is the story of the Land. "Land," says Churchill, "is the foundation of Native religious traditions. By 'land' the Natives do not just mean terrain. Land includes the beings who live on or near the Earth, the plants, animals, birds, and aquatic life; the formations of the Earth such as mountains, rocks, rivers, and lakes, and meteorological phenomena, including the winds, clouds, rain, and lightning. The entire cosmos, visible and invisible, is encompassed in the idea of Land. But Land is not an object; it consists of sentient beings, who are connected in a web of consciousness and reciprocal relationship. It is a holy thing."

Now that is a mouthful. Let's see what Churchill is really saying here, because it is central to Native American spirituality and religion. Land "is a holy thing," she tells us. As professor of world religions Harold Coward says, in the religions of the East and in the aboriginal, native religions, "the divine is usually seen as present in, rather than separate from, nature." Westerners who grew up within the matrix of Judaism, Christianity, and Islamic thinking should pause and ponder this, because it is a different view of reality. In those Western religions, as religious scholar Daniel Overmyer says: "There is just one God who exists outside the world. . . . It is really God that is sacred, not the world itself."

The experience of sacredness in the Asian and Native religions is not focused "out there"—in heaven, maybe— but right here. The world, the land, "is a holy thing." Sacredness is here and now, in this interconnected, inter- locking world in which humans are only one of the trea- sures of the "land." Native scholar Vine Deloria points out that it is a misunderstanding of the aboriginal reli- gions to say that because Mother Earth is considered sacred, she must be a Goddess. That might distance her too much from the rocks and stones and dirt that are the tabernacle of the sacred. It misses the direct "experience of personal energy within the physical universe" that the Natives experience. Some Natives say that non-Natives cannot really be experts on Native religion; they import too much separation between the terrestrial and the divine.

Another thing that is not separated in what I call the Native *sacrology* is the dignity of humans and the dignity of everything else in the cosmos. The implications of such a view are huge. Everything from air to water to plants, animals, and rocks is made of some combination of the same reality. Coward says: "There is no radical break between humans and the non-human realms of nature. . . . Exploitation of one part of nature (plants, animals, trees, etc.) by another part of nature (humans) is unacceptable." Abuse of the land, whether by overpopulation or by over- consumption, is a violation of life.

When the Natives faced the necessity of having to kill in order to eat or be protected against the elements, they did so with a paradoxical mixture of both mourning and grat- itude. They did not simply claim predator's rights. When a Kwagiutl hunter killed a bear, he would apologize and offer thanks. Before killing the bear, he would say: "Greetings, friend that we have met, only to destroy you, my friend. Apparently the creator created you so that I could hunt you to feed myself and my wife, my friend." Now the bear still dies in this scenario, but the mentality of the hunter does not make him a profligate hunter. Native Americans were stunned by the Europeans, who slaughtered whole herds without scruple or regret. They saw it as appalling arrogance, and indeed, as sacrilege. This certainly contrasts with the Western view of birds and animals as "game."

Before cutting down the hemlock tree that he needed, the tree was acknowledged, thanked, and addressed as "my friend." When a fisherman caught a salmon, he would acknowledge the salmon's sacrifice, as would his wife before cooking it. Daisy Sewid-Smith, an aboriginal writer living in Canada, says: "These practices may seem foolish to modern people, but these daily acknowledgments seem to remind the Kwagiutl that they were not the only important species on this planet."

A Wintu Native shows that this religious reverence extends even to rocks. The White man splits them and does not hear them cry. "How can the spirit of the earth like the White man? Everywhere the White man has come, the earth is sore." These rituals and ideals enforced restraints, and the Natives confessed that only humans need laws and restraints to keep them from destroying their environment. Other animals are less dangerous for Mother Earth.

Churchill and other Native American scholars are not arguing that the Natives were always ecologically sinless. They eschew romanticism of the "noble savage" sort. No people, no societies are sinless or immaculately conceived. Still, Native wisdom has remedies for Western cultural maladies.

What Is the Link between Feminism and Gratitude?

What strikes me in the Native religions is their elevation of gratitude to the top of the virtues. Their liturgies and rituals almost invariably begin with gratitude. They are thankful for the wind and the water, the plants and the trees, the fish and the animals, and for one another. Many Christian liturgies begin with repentance and confession of sin. The Natives start with exuberant thanks. Faith, hope, and charity top the Christian list of virtues. Gratitude is more basic, the Natives say. What do we have that we have not received? To be is to be a recipient. Ingratitude is almost a form of psychosis, a detachment from reality, and it is dangerous. If you don't appreciate what you've got on this generous host of an earth, or even in a personal relationship, you may lay it waste. As a species, we won't perish from a lack of information, said Abraham Heschel, but from a lack of appreciation. Gratitude is a cure for blindness. (Here the natives are close to the Buddhists with their stress on mindfulness, discussed in chapter 5.)

The absence of gratitude leads to narcissism. We lose a sense of linkage to everything else. Grateful persons can more easily see how their well-being is linked to everything else. We are tempted to think of ourselves as separate atoms. We miss that we are part of a web. Gratitude flows into a sense of interconnectedness. And this thrust in gratitude even makes scientific sense. Scientists feel that all life on earth began from a single cell. So all that lives is family, in spite of our wildly different forms. And even the first single cell that started it all was a new configuration of what started as stardust whirling in space. In fact, we are all reconfigured stardust. To recall once again the adapted Catholic mantra, "stardust thou art and unto stardust thou shalt return." The chair on which we sit, the clothes we wear, and the book we are reading can all be traced back to the primeval blast on our parent sun that rushed out into space, cooled, and became our earth. When the sun completes its mission and collapses into its "red star" phase, it and all of us will evaporate back into stardust, to be seen perhaps some time by another civilization as luminous clouds loose in space. There will be no clue left as to what we were. Native and Eastern religions are more aware of our relationship to the rest of the cosmos. That we are at all is a miracle, one that we share with the whole world. Being is a shared glory.

By now you should be wondering: How is all this going to lead to feminism? It will. But first another look at our ungrateful narcissism and how it shrinks us.

Western Euro-American cultures are marked by what Harold Coward calls an *I-self* outlook. We are, as the scholars say, individualistic. The individual is supreme. This isn't all bad. It has encouraged the defense of individual rights such as the rights to privacy and to freedom, but it has its limits. It's weak on the common good, on human solidarity, and on respect for the rest of nature. It could also contribute to a libertarian approach to reproduction: "I can have as many children as I want with no regard for the good of the community or the environment."

I-self cultures have large fault lines. Native religions in North America and elsewhere are more marked by a *we-self* outlook. They relate more to the common good and are more bonded to the other citizens of earth—the animals and the plants. Everything, including pregnancy, has a community dimension. Jacob Olupona, a scholar who studies Native African religions, was struck when he heard that during her first pregnancy, Princess Diana felt that all of England was carrying the child with her. This, says Olupona, is the experience of every woman in an African village. This sense of pregnancy as a communal event can cut two ways: It could encourage more births when the community needs that, and fewer when that is required.

So, now to the feminist connection. Gratitude has many children. One of them is humility and a lack of self-centeredness. When we see how much we owe to how many, it deflates a pretentious ego. Another offspring of gratitude is the sense of connection with the community that nourishes us. Here, community means people and the rest of nature. When the Native peoples give thanks, they thank all that is life-giving. This leads to a powerful respect for women as the unique bearers of life. Only women can bear children and nurse them into life. This appreciation could have been short-circuited, respecting women only as baby-makers. This would not be feminism. But the Natives recognize that the life-giving talents of women go beyond reproduction. As the Iroquois tradition has it: "Women are respected because they nurture the spirit of the people and remind them of their responsibilities, their kinship with all life." Women become the Clan mothers, a position of enormous responsibility. With the Mohawks, the men become chiefs, but they answer to the women, who can remove them if they fail in their duties.

As Daisy Sewid-Smith says, before the European invasion, "women had equal ranking with the men. There was no need for a feminist stand." Feminism addresses a problem that many of the Native peoples did not have. In the Native nations, there was a division of labor. Men hunted and were the warriors, but women managed the village and the agriculture. Debra Lynn White Plume writes about the Lakota people: Before the invasion, "adult men and women existed as equal human beings. . . . Men and women each held definite roles in society that were considered of equal importance to the Nation." Different roles did not mean inequality. A Papago woman explained with confident humor to anthropologist Ruth Underhill, "Don't you see that without us there would be no men? Why should we envy men? We made men."

Churchill tells us that "as a result of this equality, domestic violence rarely occurred in Indian families. Instead, men and women participated in all spheres of society including the family." In the Cherokee and the Iroquois cultures, the home belonged to the women, and the children belonged to the mother's clan. Churchill says: "The most important male in a child's life in this case was the clan uncle (the mother's brother), not the child's father. This arrangement not only secured women's authority in the home but it enabled failed marriages to dissolve without significant harm to the children."

It is not surprising, therefore, that Native communities tended to have appropriate population size. When women are empowered, that is the usual result. This is a lesson the world is slowly learning.

Application to Family Planning

Prior to the assault on Native culture, there were many customs that wisely addressed the need for the empowerment of women, especially but not exclusively in the area of family planning. In 1998, an event happened that was a moment of major recovery. Eleven Dakota girls "lived alone" for the first time in over a century. Guided by their female elders, these "child-beloveds" participated in a ceremony that had been prohibited by the U.S. government for five generations: the *Ishna Ti Awica Dowan*, or "singing for those who live alone." It was in the 1880s that this coming-of-age puberty ceremony became a crime under the Indian Offenses policy. Only with the passage of the American Indian Religious Freedom Act in 1978 could this ceremony be publicly and legally practiced.

Now, as Churchill tells us, "Dakota girls once again became women in the traditional way." The traditional way stressed strength, self-respect, and the authority and responsibilities of women in Dakota culture. These rites, taught by older women, gave young girls a sense of their natural right to manage their sexual and reproductive lives. They also stressed an important theme in most Native cultures, the pursuit of harmony with all of nature.

In other ways also, adolescent girls were helped toward sexual and reproductive maturity. Churchill says: "Through stories elders warn girls about the dangers of men." These stories continued the instruction on the need for women to manage their sexuality. Mothers were especially vigilant. In Lakota culture, according to Lame Deer: "If you were a tipi-creeper you'd find out that mothers had a habit of tying a hair rope around their daughter's waists, passing it through their legs. This was a 'No Trespassing' sign. If a boy was found fooling around with that rope, the women would burn his tipi down or kill his horse."

Native cultures showed a keen awareness of the need to restrain sexual impulse and reproduction. Virginity was given status, and periods of celibacy were built into daily life as ceremonial requirements. Girls were to retreat to the menstrual hut for some three or four days to be alone. Says Churchill: "It was a ceremonial occasion which enabled a woman to get in touch with her own special power."

Sleeping separately was a form of birth control in the past. One Dakota woman reported: "Mother and father never slept together, men and women slept on different sides of lodges. Maybe we have to do that again." As a woman of the Ojibwe people said: "It is a disgrace to have children like steps and stairs. If a man had sense, he didn't bother his wife while a child was young." In a way that resembles Chinese traditions, some nations taught that sexual energy is a limited quotient. A man of strong character would restrain himself to preserve his sexual energy and also to be able to concentrate on the child he has before siring another.

These customs emitted many signals of responsibility regarding sex and family planning. In Native cultures, family planning made sense. Churchill sums this up: In spite of the great diversity in the many Native North American cultures and religions, they unite on "the privileging of the common good, the belief in the sacrality of Mother Earth, and the interrelatedness of all life." Native Americans know from their own experience that too much reproduction can violate these beliefs. Coward says that all the world's major religions "have encouraged population growth in irresponsible ways" except for Buddhism, the Chinese religions (Taoism and Confucianism), and the aboriginal, Native religions.

Native religions saw that you can't respect Mother Earth without family planning. The North American natives also learned the need for family planning from their own mistakes—a major route to wisdom for us all. There are many cases, for example, in the Southwest when overpopulation imposed excessive burdens on the communities and the fragile desert environments. The Native oral traditions teach lessons about this in their stories. The Cherokee story on the origin of disease, for example, says that animals introduced afflictions into the world because humans were overpopulating the earth and treating animals carelessly. In the Navajo account of creation, Coyote warns the people: "If we all live, and continue to increase as we have done, the earth will soon be too small to hold us, and there will be no room for the cornfields."

Churchill says that "Native traditional knowledge of practices of birth control also indicate concern with population size. These sources suggest that prior to European contact, Native people generally strived to live in harmony with their environment, balancing their population size with the resources available in their regions." As much as they valued sexuality, they saw the need for limits. Sexual abstinence was prescribed for men and women who were seeking spiritual growth. Warriors, hunters, and others in some societies had to practice abstinence; and the times for abstinence varied from four days to four weeks, four months, or even four years.

Contraception and abortion have been practiced in Native communities, and women have authority here. Churchill says, "men did not interfere with women's matters, especially concerning sexuality. Women therefore traditionally make their own decision about family planning, contraception and abortion, all of which have been practiced in American Indian societies, to a greater or lesser degree." A contemporary group called the Native Women for Reproductive Rights Coalition explains the common attitude of Native women: "Within traditional societies and languages, there is no word that equals abortion. The word itself is harsh and impersonal. When speaking to traditional elders knowledgeable about reproductive health matters, repeatedly they would refer to a woman knowing which herbs and methods to use 'to make her period come.' This was seen as a woman taking care of herself and doing what was necessary."

Lakota women maintain their traditional authority over their bodies. "Anything that has to do with our bodies . . . is really our business as women, and as Lakota women, it is part of our culture to make our own decision about abortion. . . . It is our privilege as Lakota women to make decisions about our bodies." A 1991 Women of Color Reproductive Health Poll showed that many Native women hold this philosophy. They found that 80 percent of Native American women believe every woman should decide for herself whether or not to have an abortion.

"Savage Rites and Heathenish Customs"

In the 1880s, the Courts of Indian Offenses tribunal set out to eliminate the "savage" customs of the Natives. The best that can be said of these courts is that they did recognize that they were dealing with a different culture, one that was more ecologically sophisticated and highly advanced in giving equal rights to women and men—and therefore a serious threat to the invading culture. The lesson from Native cultures is that family planning, including abortion as a backup when necessary, need not be controversial. The "abortion wars" of Western cultures today occur in a context in which nature is not our mother but is the raw material for our greed, and in which women are suppressed and therefore feared. Our Western cultures are also riven with tensions between fear of sex on one hand and pornographic obsession on the other. We do not enjoy a peaceful possession of our sexuality. In such an unhealthy climate, sane discussions of family planning are hard to come by, and the battle lines are drawn.

Conclusion

OUR WORLD'S PROBLEMS ARE ENORMOUS and interlocking. Our greed, in the observation of Christian ethics professor Larry Rasmussen, has turned life into an emergency. The solution to the mess we're in cannot be merely technical. After studying the perils of too much growth, scientist Jorgen Randers concluded: "Probably only religion has the moral force to bring about [the necessary] change."

In 1990, thirty-four renowned scientists led by Carl Sagan and Hans Bethe wrote an appeal to the religions of the world. Their position was that "efforts to safeguard and cherish" this battered earth "need to be infused with a vision of the sacred." Religion has been part of the problem. It has to be part of the solution. The Catholic Cardinal John Henry Newman said that people will die for a dogma (a religious conviction) who will not stir for a conclusion. Nothing so stirs the human will as the tincture of the sacred. The problems presented by greedy overconsumption, the human incapacity to share, and overpopulation require a reshaping of the human spirit, a kind of moral heart transplant. All the religions we studied are into this kind of heart transplantation. They have had successes in the past and have helped in our tortuous limping toward civilization, but they never faced a challenge like this.

In this book, we have seen the wisdom of multiple religions and cultures on the broad issues underlying family planning. As with the travelers in *The Canterbury Tales*, each has a story to tell and wisdom to share. If our ears are open, conversations with these cultures can be medicinal. Each of these religious traditions show strong respect for the gift of children, and each of them sees fertility as a blessing. Each of them also sees it as a potential curse.

Family planning is not a radical idea. It is simply the service we owe this earth, an earth that is, in novelist Alan Paton's words, "lovely beyond any singing of it." No one could say that our "abortion wars" are normal or represent humanity at its best. Maybe some of the peace of these other cultures who faced the same questions can quietly seep into our souls. This may seem an unlikely dream, but to adapt the words of the Irish poet William Butler Yeats, tread softly if you would tread upon that dream.

Bandarage, Asoka. *Women, Population, and Global Crisis.* ZedBooks, 1997.

Brown, Lester R. *Who Will Feed China?* W. W. Norton, 1995.

Cohen, Jeremy. *"Be Fertile and Increase, Fill the Earth and Master It": The Ancient and Medieval Career of a Biblical Text.* Cornell University Press, 1989.

Cohen, Joel E. *How Many People Can the Earth Support?* Norton, 1995.

Coward, Harold and Daniel C. Maguire, eds. *Visions of a New Earth: Religious Perspectives on Population, Consumption, and Ecology.* State University of New York Press, 2000.

Coward, Harold, ed. *Population, Consumption, and the Environment: Religious and Secular Responses.* State University of New York Press, 1995.

Dombrowski, Daniel A. and Robert Deltete. *A Brief, Liberal Catholic Defense of Abortion.* University of Illinois Press, 2000.

Hartmann, Betsy. *Reproductive Rights and Wrongs: The Global Politics of Population Control.* South End Press, 1987.

LaFleur, William R. *Liquid Life: Abortion and Buddhism in Japan.* Princeton University Press, 1992.

Maguire, Daniel C. and Larry L. Rasmussen. *Ethics for a Small Planet: New Horizons on Population, Consumption, and Ecology.* State University of New York Press, 1998.

Maguire, Daniel C. *Sacred Energies: When the World's Religions Sit Down to Talk about the Future of Human Life and the Plight of This Planet.* Fortress Press, 2000.

Ponting, Clive. *A Green History of the World: The Environment and the Collapse of Great Civilizations.* Penguin Books, 1991.

Steffen, Lloyd. *Abortion: A Reader.* Pilgrim Press, 1996.